Classic

WOODEN MOTOR

Yachts

*W*ooden boats. They are the cherished relic bones of forest giants: breathing towers of living water that burst from the earth when Arthur was king and scrambled heavenward toward the sun. They are the blacksmith's forge, the weaver's loom, the shipwright's chest, and the draftsman's dream. They are replanked, reframed, and refastened with stainless determination and then preserved with paint, varnish, and callused pride. They are each an ark of primordial secrets: living things within the water that are conceived in tradition and perpetually reanimated by love."

—CHUCK GOULD, NOR'WESTING

*A*ntique' is it? Who cares that you were built in 1893 just across the bay? What matters is your strength, the strength of oak and fir and teak, of hackmatack knees and locust treenails that alternate with bronze.

" 'Decrepit,' they say—too old to keep the sea. Well, you served the pilots for fifty-two years just beyond the Bar. Winter and summer, blow high, blow low, you lived out there with the sea all wild when gales came roaring in. Nothing could put you down. Save progress.

" 'Obsolete,' . . . you'll be obsolete when the oceans drain and the winds no longer blow."

—STERLING HAYDEN, WANDERER

A dead ship, dumped by an owner too impatient and cheap and unimaginative and law-abiding to know how to make her seaworthy again; a ship that was only acting dead, just waiting for someone to come along, recognize her true worth, and rescue her from scrap."

—FRANCISCO GOLDMAN, THE ORDINARY SEAMAN

Classic
WOODEN MOTOR
Yachts

RON MCCLURE

INTERNATIONAL MARINE/MCGRAW HILL

Camden, Maine | New York | Chicago | San Francisco | Lisbon | London | Madrid | Mexico City
Milan | New Delhi | San Juan | Seoul | Singapore | Sydney | Toronto

Contents

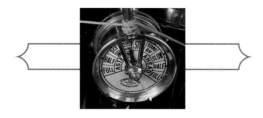

For Kathy

Introduction

It usually happens in a heartbeat. You're walking the docks in the quiet evening sun, ambling through a floating maze of plastic and reflective chrome. Suddenly, you see a boat like no other in the entire marina: a wooden beauty, marvelously unique. It pulls you like a magnet. Your eyes narrow as you inspect the old-fashioned design: part Model A, part *African Queen.* Antique violin in color, she's full of burnished-bronze deck fittings and fancy knotted stanchions. You want to touch the boat, slide your hand over her varnished teak rails. When the owner peers out through lace curtains, surrounded by brass kerosene lamps, you can't help asking the obvious, "Is this a classic?"

The term *classic* has become a cliché—it's applied to everything from a can of Coke to a fiberglass MG replica. Even dedicated boating enthusiasts argue about what constitutes a classic. The Classic Yacht Association defines *classic* as a pleasure boat built before World War II, made of wood and still true to her original design. Yet, in this book, you'll find other boats as well: workboats, tugboats, boats built after World War II, and some that are not made entirely of wood. The photographs and stories that fill each chapter will help you understand—as I have over the years—what makes these, and hundreds of other boats, classic.

After reading this book and gazing at the color photographs, you'll understand that the term *classic* does not mean just a type or genre or period; it connotes something much more: it's a process. And you'll begin to appreciate that boats become classics because of the love, sweat, and tears that go into them over the decades. It's a moniker hard earned, hard maintained, and always presented with pride and affection by a loosely affiliated subculture of wooden-boat aficionados who understand the concept because they are the essence of it. It's not just about the boats. Classic yachting is a way of life and, once smitten (often in a heartbeat), you're forever netted.

I would like to thank the following people for their gracious help with and enthusiasm for this project: David and Ruth Gillespie, Earl McMillen III, Mike and Peggy O'Brien, Martin McNair, Dave Walker, Dorin Robinson, Mel and Gig Owen, and Julian Matson.

Allure

MARTIN AND JANIS McNAIR

San Rafael, California

Recently, while loitering in a used-book store, I upended a paperback entitled *1,000 Boat Names*. Browsing its pages was like strolling the docks of an all-fiberglass marina with every nautical word concoction and inventive spelling imaginable represented. However, this trend in cute and creative names for boats was (thankfully) a phenomenon not in vogue during the decades when classic yachts were built. Wooden boat owners take the name of their boat quite seriously, evidenced by a visit to any wooden boat festival or reading any of the classic wooden boat books. The name of a precious wooden boat is something one considers at length—it should be meaningful and should endure the test of time—just as the craft that bears it. And few boats are more aptly named than Martin and Janis McNair's *Allure*.

Built in 1931 by Stephens Brothers Boat Builders at its yard in Stockton, California, *Allure* was purchased by her first owner for the sum of $12,567. Martin notes that, to the best of his knowledge, the boat spent her early years plying the San Francisco Delta and Bay areas, and somehow managed to escape conscription into the navy during World War II. *Allure* is considered a standard raised-deck cruiser—meaning that her forward deck is slightly higher than her side and aft decks—and she was configured in the

typical Stephens layout of two heads, two sleeping compartments, a pilothouse, and a galley.

When he and Janis purchased *Allure*, Martin admits that they searched long and hard for the right classic. They saw her at the San Rafael docks and courted the owners (who had been married aboard *Allure*) for some time. Martin adds that *Allure* was in very solid condition when they purchased her.

"The engines were sound, as was the hull, so we were able

to spend our time and energies on cosmetics and minor interior modifications for comfort," says Martin.

And comfort is clearly evident as you step aboard this unique boat. Her forward cabin, with a small head, includes two berths with plenty of storage drawers beneath. The port-size berth is a cozy but adequate double. The white-painted woodwork and brightly colored linens, pillows, and curtains—all well lit from the butterfly skylight overhead—make this cabin cheery and attractive.

On the starboard side, the pilothouse is roomy, with a drop-leaf table behind the steering station to port and a two-place settee. The galley and main cabin are accessed from starboard, and the head is located opposite the portside galley amidships. Next is a comfortable aft cabin, with a couch to starboard that converts to a double bunk below and a single bunk above. The McNairs exchanged the port berth for a small dinette area and removed the bulkhead between the galley and the aft cabin to create a larger and more open feeling. The results complement the boat well.

With the Chrysler twin engines, *Allure* easily attains 18 knots in flat water; however, she cruises comfortably and relatively economically at 10 knots. Since becoming the caretakers in 1990, the McNairs have hosted three weddings aboard *Allure* and have been the lead boat in the opening-day parade of boating season in San Francisco Bay.

Topsides, *Allure* is sparkling. The handrails appear to be part of her decks, creating a streamlined appearance. One of her most comfortable hangouts, the covered aft cockpit, easily seats four people. The side steps exiting the cockpit also function as storage and seats and still retain their original bronze Stephens lids. This boat has earned her name, epitomizing the classic allure that draws admirers and enthusiasts, as well as embodying the commitment of wooden boat owners to the care and stewardship that keep boats like *Allure* alive for posterity.

Allure

YEAR:	1931
DESIGNER:	Stephens Brothers Boat Builders
BUILDER:	Stephens Brothers Boat Builders, Stockton, California
LENGTH:	43 feet
BEAM:	10 feet, 6 inches
DRAFT:	3 feet
ORIGINAL POWER:	Twin Scripps, gasoline
CURRENT POWER:	Twin Chrysler Marine 318, gasoline
CONSTRUCTION:	Cedar planking over oak frames, teak superstructure
HOME PORT:	San Rafael, California

Annie Laurie

BARRY WHITE

Chester, Connecticut

Annie Laurie is a big, roomy, and comfortable original cruiser. Her current owner, Barry White, has lived aboard full time since the mid-1980s, sharing this beautiful vessel with his family. According to Barry, *Annie Laurie* was built for Frederick L. Putnam of Boston and was launched in 1929 at the Gray Boat Works in Thomaston, Maine. Originally named *Gladlar*, she spent her summers during the 1930s as an elegant commuter shuttle, transporting Putnam from his summer home in Marblehead, Massachusetts, to his Boston office. During the winter, *Gladlar* was berthed in West Palm Beach, Florida. She was always maintained by a full-time captain and steward.

Like hundreds of other marvelous pleasure boats on America's coastlines, *Gladlar* was called into service by the armed forces during World War II. According to Barry's research, she was stationed off Cape Cod, Massachusetts, on a rotation of nine days out and five days in, acting as a U-boat patrol vessel.

After the war, Putnam repurchased the boat from the coast guard and returned her to her berths in Marblehead and West Palm Beach. After he died in the late 1970s, the boat changed hands several times, eventually

Annie Laurie

YEAR:	1929
DESIGNER:	Albert Condon
BUILDER:	Gray Boat Works, Thomaston, Maine
LENGTH:	60 feet
BEAM:	13 feet
DRAFT:	4 feet
ORIGINAL POWER:	Twin Sterling Dolphin, gasoline
CURRENT POWER:	Twin GM 671, diesel
CONSTRUCTION:	Double-planked mahogany over white-oak frames, mahogany cabin, teak decks
HOME PORT:	Chester, Connecticut

falling into a state of disrepair and neglect. In 1980, she was purchased by Janice Schmidt in Mystic, Connecticut, and was renamed *Annie Laurie*. Barry purchased her from Schmidt in 1985.

The interior of *Annie Laurie* is fun and functional. The forepeak contains a V-berth with a crawl-through entry—a perfect haven for youngsters. Located abaft this space is a second sleeping cabin, with a bunk and storage cabinets to port and a built-in writing desk with seating opposite. Steps lead up to a large saloon area with dining table, built-in seating, cabinets, and a cozy wood-burning stove. A full galley amidships is abaft the saloon and accessed by a short hallway to starboard, which leads to the raised pilothouse with a small captain's cabin. Farther aft is the master stateroom, complete with an enclosed head.

Topsides, *Annie Laurie* is just as comfortable and functional as below, with the luxury of walkaround decks, a full canopy over the aft deck space, and a large, open lounging area aft.

Barry began an extensive restoration in 1985, intent on returning *Annie Laurie* as closely as possible to her original condition—efforts that are now clearly evident. Moored at Chester, Connecticut, *Annie Laurie* cruises on Long Island Sound and has twice cruised to Ottawa, Canada, via the Erie and Radieu Canals. She has traveled the Hudson River and the Intracoastal Waterway as far south as the Carolinas.

Belle

ELIZABETH AND EARL MCMILLEN III AND CHUCK PARRISH, MANAGERS

Newport, Rhode Island

*I*t's 8 A.M. on a clear and magnificent summer morning at the tiny airport outside Newport, Rhode Island. I'm buckled into the cockpit of a vintage Beechcraft Bonanza. My wife Kathy is behind me, sandwiched between a new Yamaha outboard engine and several boxes of supplies. We're about to take off for Martha's Vineyard to photograph the 1929 classic Launch, *Belle*. Her owner, Earl McMillen, is at the controls. We taxi and rise, lumping through the updrafts, and then bank over the harbors and marinas. Newport and the surrounding oceanside communities are a boat lover's paradise—I've never seen so many boats on a bay. Earl banks the plane sharply against the sun, flying south along the beach to point out the famous Gatsby-esque mansions along Bellevue Avenue. Then we climb and Earl heads us out to sea, east to another tiny airstrip on the island of Martha's Vineyard.

I'd seen pictures of *Belle* on Earl's Web site, and I'm eager to see her firsthand and have the privilege of boarding her. But when I finally see her, I'm left speechless. This 77-foot varnished mahogany pleasure yacht is as pristine and perfectly detailed both inside and out as the day she was built.

Owned briefly by country-western singer-songwriter David Allen Coe, *Belle* spent much of her life in the South, in Florida and North

Carolina. Built in 1929—the year the stock market crashed—by the New York Yacht, Launch & Engine Company of Morris Heights, *Belle* was originally named *Madge III*. Her hull is planked with Douglas fir over steam-bent oak frames, and she was powered with twin six-cylinder 100-horsepower 20th Century gasoline engines. She was the prototype for many of the boats that NYYL&E produced but, like many yachts during the unstable 1930s, she went from owner to owner. By 1934, she had been acquired by a man in Norfolk, Virginia, and became a "southern belle."

We step from the small launch that has ferried us out from the harbor at Martha's Vineyard onto her beautiful teak and bronze swinging gangway and are greeted by her captain, Craig Callahan, and chef Hannah Troggis. They are largely responsible for the boat's pristine condition. Her teak decks are almost pure white and stunning against the varnished Honduras mahogany cabinsides and caprails. *Belle*'s immediate attraction is the spa-cious aft deck, shaded under taut canvas and mahogany ribs. With wicker lounge chairs and a full-beam cushioned seat at the stern, this deck is more like an open-air saloon. This section of the boat is enhanced by a small fishing or boarding cockpit abaft the aft seating area, accessible by a companionway that opens from center and steps down.

The cabins below are accessed via a companionway amidships, just aft of the pilothouse. The quarters are spacious, beautiful, and original. Accessed from either side, the pilothouse is small and designed for captains only. It overlooks the formal dining area, which is reached through a companionway to starboard. This elegant cabin showcases the extravagance and opulence of the Roaring Twenties: the joinery work and paneling, the hand-carved furniture, the drapes framing massive opening sash windows, and the tastefully placed antiques.

Earl tells us that during the spring and fall, *Belle* cruises the Georgia and South Carolina coasts, and southern Florida and the Bahamas in the winter months. The boat's summer cruising areas are primarily the coastal waters of southern New England and Maine. "She calls at Nantucket and Martha's Vineyard frequently, where one of my partners in the boat, Chuck Parrish, keeps a summer house."

Although it's difficult to believe, *Belle* lives outside year-round. Her condition is equal to any classic we've seen—most of which spend sheltered lives under covered moorage. Earl explains that the boat wasn't always in such excellent condition, however. "She was a complete basket case, with oysters growing in the bilges and a worm-ridden keel when I found her." *Belle* was fully restored by McMillen Yachts Inc. in 1998.

Moving around her decks above and below, I find it impossible to stop shooting pictures—every inch, every detail is so classic wooden yacht. Eventually, we have to leave; as we pull away in the open launch in a lively midday chop, *Belle*'s hull rises above us. She is more ship than I expected, yet she possesses all the grace and charm any classic yacht owner could want.

Soon we are again climbing sharply in the Beechcraft. The reflection of the sun plays on the harbor below. We gaze down at *Belle* one final time before flying westward from Martha's Vineyard toward Newport.

Belle

YEAR:	1929
DESIGNER:	New York Yacht, Launch & Engine Company Morris Heights, New York
BUILDER:	New York Yacht, Launch & Engine Company Morris Heights, New York
LENGTH:	77 feet
BEAM:	16 feet
DRAFT:	4 feet
ORIGINAL POWER:	Twin 20th Century, gasoline
CURRENT POWER:	Twin Caterpillar 3116 Turbo, diesel
CONSTRUCTION:	Douglas fir over steam-bent oak
HOME PORT:	Newport, Rhode Island

Capolavoro

Bob Lamson

Seattle, Washington

"I was in Venice, Italy, on vacation," says Bob Lamson, "admiring the blown-glass works and riding in the water taxies when I saw one of these beautiful boats."

Bob says there are literally hundreds of water taxis cruising the canals in Venice, but very few of them are wooden.

"When I went back to my hotel, I couldn't get the boat I'd seen out of my mind. When I described it to the concierge, he actually knew the man who had built it, and he called him."

Elio Salvagno is one of the few boatbuilders left who is currently producing wooden boats for very discerning customers. When Bob went to see Salvagno at his boatyard, two boats were under construction.

"One had just been completed," Bob says. "The other was just being started. I was able to see the level of craftsmanship that went into the boats, plus the end product."

Although he had no intention of owning such a boat, by the time he returned home, Bob could think of nothing else. "It was like a sudden addiction," Bob says, laughing at the memory. "I couldn't keep myself from calling and having one of those boats commissioned."

Bob has been told that the Venice water taxis provided the design for

Capolavoro

YEAR:	1999
DESIGNER:	Elio Salvagno, Cantiere Motonautico Serenella, Venice, Italy
BUILDER:	Elio Salvagno, Cantiere Motonautico Serenella, Venice, Italy
LENGTH:	29 feet
BEAM:	7 feet, 6 inches
DRAFT:	2 feet
POWER:	Volvo-Penta I/O, diesel
CONSTRUCTION:	Cold-molded South African mahogany, teak floors, walnut trim
HOME PORT:	Seattle, Washington

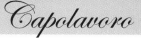

the original PT boats of World War II. "Their maneuverability at slow speeds is amazing. Plus, they do great in any kind of chop or beam sea. Their sharp V-bow and flat stern, plus the fact that they draw very little water, produce a steady, smooth ride, with little or no roll."

According to Bob, one of *Capolavoro*'s best features is the cockpit design. "The boat runs very quiet. You can be at 35 knots and carry on a normal conversation."

For Bob, the best thing about the boat is her aesthetics. The boat's African-mahogany construction and hand-polished hull, coupled with her beautiful handcrafted walnut, teak, and ash interior, make her a Venetian work of art. The boat can easily carry up to ten passengers; however, its true calling is to provide an intimate evening for two on the lake. The low-ceilinged comfortable saloon is ideal for lounging and enjoying cocktails while adrift. The transparent cabin roof slides open on warm nights or beads in a light Seattle rain.

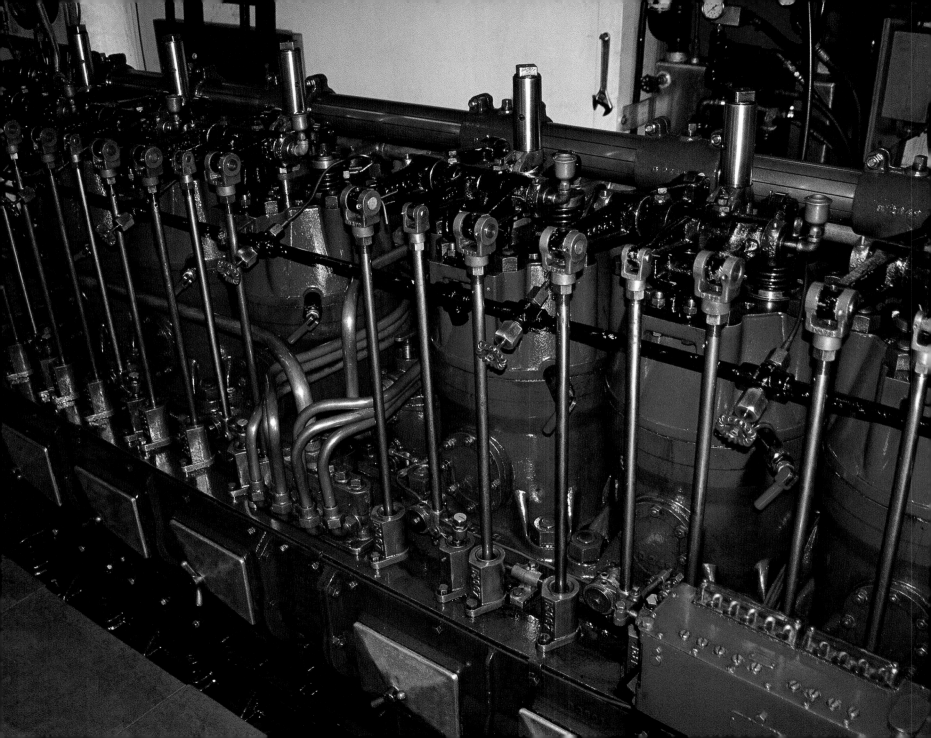

Catalyst

HUGH REILLY, PACIFIC CATALYST EXPEDITIONS, L.L.C.

Port Townsend, Washington

Built in 1932 by Lake Union Dry Dock of Seattle from a design by prominent naval architects Roland & Strictland, *Catalyst* was the brainchild of Thomas G. Thompson, a professor at the University of Washington. According to current owner, Hugh Reilly, it was Thompson's dream to establish a school of oceanography at the university; a Rockefeller grant enabled him to commission the construction of a boat to be used as the school's research vessel.

"Thompson was set on owning a vessel that would meet the needs of the scientists who would use her," says Hugh, "and when completed, *Catalyst* was considered the most state-of-the-art vessel of her day."

After rolling down the ways in 1932, her maiden voyage was a cruise through the Inside Passage and across the Gulf of Alaska. *Catalyst* spent the next eleven years collecting scientific data in the Puget Sound area—the foundation of scientific understanding of those waters today. In 1942, *Catalyst* was conscripted into the war effort; a machine gun was mounted on her pilothouse, depth chargers were set on her stern, and she spent the war years patrolling the Aleutian Islands of Alaska.

After the war, she was sold as surplus. Purchased by an Alaskan mining company, *Catalyst* underwent a major refit. The main cabin, originally

separated from the pilothouse, was extended forward and the wheelhouse was placed on top of it. Large hatches were created forward and aft. Until she was sold two years later, *Catalyst* was used to transport tungsten ore. During the next forty years, various owners used the boat for many purposes—from a mail carrier to a floating dental office—calling on ports as far away as Baja California, Hawaii, and Alaska.

Today, *Catalyst* is a floating tribute to the foresight and determination of her more recent owners and people like Hugh Reilly, who understand the value of maintaining historical ves-

sels in a manner that respects their originality, the period of their construction, and the purpose of their design. *Catalyst* is still the salty workboat, running on the same Estep diesel, that Thomas G. Thompson envisioned in 1932.

The engine room is amazing: a power plant housed in a complex floating workshop. The main saloon, with its large dining table, leads forward to a unique and attractive galley, with a second spacious dining area forward. Abaft the saloon are a head and a cabin with a double bunk. Like her sister ship, the *Westward* (see page 175), *Catalyst* has marvelous deck space for passengers to use for strolling, photographing, or relaxing. The aft and side decks are covered from the stern to the forward bulkhead of the main cabin, a welcome feature for cruising in the Pacific Northwest.

Below decks, the holds that once carried tungsten ore

Catalyst

YEAR:	1932
DESIGNER:	Roland & Strictland, Seattle, Washington
BUILDER:	Lake Union Dry Dock Company, Seattle, Washington
LENGTH:	74 feet, 7 inches
BEAM:	18 feet, 4 inches
DRAFT:	9 feet, 4 inches
ORIGINAL POWER:	Washington Estep, diesel
CURRENT POWER:	Same
CONSTRUCTION:	Double-planked Alaska yellow cedar over oak frames
HOME PORT:	Port Townsend, Washington

have been converted to simple yet attractive and comfortable staterooms that can accommodate twelve people. The pilot-house is completely original, and the exterior side decks provide easy access to the life rafts, skiffs, and kayaks stored atop the main cabin.

On a cold and windy fall day in Port Townsend, Kathy and I were invited aboard both the *Westward* and the *Catalyst* for a day cruise. The owner graciously enlisted full crews to operate each boat and even provided a skiff to ferry me between them while on the open waters of Puget Sound. We enjoyed lounging inside and strolling the decks, falling in love with both boats: the feeling of comfort and security underway, the unique blend of roominess and coziness, the quiet operation, and the clear vistas from every area of the boat. I was fascinated with the idea that both boats continue their original purpose from three quarters of a century ago: carrying passengers north through the Puget Sound, Gulf Islands, and Inside Passage to Southeast Alaska.

Chyma L

JIM AND CHYMA SMITH

Olympia, Washington

*I*f the original builders and designers at the Owens Yacht Company in Baltimore, Maryland, could see the *Chyma L* today, they would be delighted and proud. Her rebirth, after decades of neglect, has resulted in a most attractive family cruiser that would appeal to any wooden boat lover.

Jim Smith explains that he and his wife Chyma enjoy long after-dinner walks around their hometown of Olympia, Washington. "One evening, we noticed this little boat sitting in a boatyard that we often walk past. This was back in 1998. She really had a classic look that appealed to us."

The engines had been removed and the boat was in very poor condition. After six months of walking by her and seeing no indication of any owner attention, Jim finally stopped and inquired. "The yard owner was quite upset. The Owens was taking up yard space, and he hadn't heard from her owners in months."

After contacting the owner, Jim cut a deal for $1,400 plus the delinquent storage fees. He had the boat trucked to his backyard, where the restoration efforts would commence. "I started by stripping all the ugly carpet and wallpaper out of the interior," Jim says. "Next went the Formica countertops."

Jim soon discovered areas of rot in the hull and the forepeak. At that

point, he contacted a marine surveyor, and the restoration project proceeded in earnest. During the next two years, planks were replaced on the starboard side and in the bow areas. The boat was totally rewired, replumbed, refastened, and repowered. The interior was completely gutted and restored to its original mahogany configuration. Original seats found for the dinette area were reupholstered.

"I bought another abandoned Owens and salvaged many original parts that I needed," Jim says.

Jim located a third identical Owens that still contained the original engines, transmissions, gauges, and cables. He was able to purchase all the mechanical parts for $1,500. Although both engines were seized, this presented no problem for Jim: for most of his life, he has been rebuilding and restoring classic cars and pickup trucks. "I rebuilt everything—the motors, starters, carburetors, and Jabsco 777 saltwater pumps."

The list of upgrades continues on this 30-foot gem, but most important is the way Jim retained the original makeup of

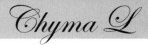

the boat—perhaps the result of his lifelong interest in restoring cars and his ability to find original parts. Unlike prewar cruisers that were frequently one-of-a-kind boats built by yards that have long since disappeared, *Chyma L* is actually a production-line cruiser, which makes it possible to find parts boats. Yet, to see this boat, it's difficult to imagine that she came off an assembly line.

"The restoration started as a three- to five-year project," Jim says. "About seven months after buying the boat, we ran into a great deal on a boathouse, but it had to be occupied within six months. Needless to say, this bumped up our timetable, and we were able to occupy the boathouse by August of 2000."

Jim and Chyma plan to cruise the Puget Sound until their retirement, and then head north for Canadian waters. Every spring, *Chyma L* can be seen firsthand at the Wooden Boat Festival in Olympia, Washington.

Chyma L

YEAR:	1960
DESIGNER:	Owens Yacht Company, Baltimore, Maryland
BUILDER:	Owens Yacht Company, Baltimore, Maryland
LENGTH:	30 feet
BEAM:	10 feet, 8 inches
DRAFT:	2 feet, 6 inches
ORIGINAL POWER:	Twin Flagships
CURRENT POWER:	Twin Flagship Model 185, Chevrolet Marine
CONSTRUCTION:	Double-planked mahogany hull, teak decks, mahogany interior
HOME PORT:	Olympia, Washington

Cleodoxa

Rob Fox

Cowichan Bay, British Columbia

Cowichan Bay is not on the beaten path—a narrow road winds down to a sheltered bay, cutting deep against a steep cliff. Most of the shops and businesses are built on poles over the tide flats. I visited during the maritime festival, and hundreds of people were enjoying the boat-building contests, artists painting on the wooden docks, a Native People's museum, and dozens of craft stalls. I had made no formal arrangement with the owner of *Cleodoxa*, but when I asked a waitress at his café, she just smiled and pointed toward the water.

"Walk out on the docks as far as you can and you'll see this really old, creaky boat. It's real skinny," she said. "Rob's inside, I think. They just got done playing."

Envision a remote fishing and lumbering camp on the eastern shore of Vancouver Island—bereft of Holiday Inns and McDonald's restaurants —home port to hundreds of small wooden workboats, fishing boats, and sailboats (as well as a few fiberglass cruisers). *Cleodoxa* is a classic wooden yacht that clearly stands out in the midst of all of these unique wooden vessels. Her owner, an affable man named Rob Fox, was relaxing with his buddies, just as the waitress predicted.

"We just got done playing a gig," he said, inviting my wife Kathy and me aboard. "I play French horn in a brass ensemble. We just played a concert for the festival."

The boat is beyond unique. Shaped like a banana that lists to port or starboard (depending on how she got up that day),

she is like a feisty dowager who has kept to herself for the better part of a century, watching and waiting as the world around her slowly changes.

"I climbed aboard the boat for the first time twenty-six years ago," says Rob. "Sat down right there on that comfortable portside

couch, looked around at her interior, and knew without question that this was the boat I would own for the rest of my life."

The aft cockpit is perfect: furnished with cushions for seating, covered by a hard canopy with roll-up canvas curtains, decorated with live plants, and accented with burnished-bronze hardware and beautifully varnished teak caprails.

Built in 1912 in Vancouver, British Columbia, by A. W. LaPage at his Gasoline Engine Company shipyard, the boat was christened *Yrrebeinna* (the mirrored name of the builder's wife). The original power was a 15-horsepower two-cylinder gasoline engine located in the boat's forepeak. In 1922, a prominent Vancouver resident named W. C. Shelly bought and renamed her *Cora-Marie*. However, by 1924, Shelly decided that he wanted a larger boat, so he had the Hoffar-Beeching yard literally cut her in half and add 7 feet to her midsection. Shelly also had the boat repowered with a 60-horsepower Scripps four-cylinder air-start engine mounted amidships. By 1926, Shelly wanted an even

Cleodoxa

YEAR:	1912
DESIGNER:	A. W. LaPage, Vancouver, British Columbia
BUILDER:	A. W. LaPage, Vancouver, British Columbia
LENGTH:	54 feet length overall
BEAM:	9 feet, 6 inches
DRAFT:	4 feet, 6 inches
ORIGINAL POWER:	Gasoline, built by the Sam Jones Company
CURRENT POWER:	4-cylinder Isuzu, diesel
CONSTRUCTION:	Douglas-fir planking over oak frames, teak house
HOME PORT:	Cowichan, British Columbia

larger vessel, and he sold his boat—taking the name with him to be used on his next yacht, the 107-foot *Cora-Marie*, which was launched in 1929.

Lengthened and repowered but nameless, *Cleodoxa* was purchased by R. J. Sprott, founder of the Sprott Shaw Schools in Vancouver. Sprott named her *Cleodoxa* after one of the slain daughters of Niobe, Queen of Thebes, from Greek mythology.

In the ensuing decade of Prohibition, *Cleodoxa* became an interesting player in the flourishing trade of running rum between Canada and the United States. Bruce Arundel, an electronics instructor at the Sprott Shaw School, was charged with the task of inventing a communications system that was easier to use than Morse code, yet could not be picked up by the U.S. Coast Guard. Arundel and coinventor Ed Chisholm developed the first radio-telephone, which they installed and tested aboard *Cleodoxa.*

In the following decades, *Cleodoxa* changed owners several times, but never lost her name. Rob Fox discovered her in 1976, when there wasn't an inch of teak showing on the boat—everything had been covered with red and white paint. Moving aboard, Fox began a thorough restoration, restoring her splendid teak brightwork as well as other improvements.

"She had a Ford gas engine in her when I bought her," says Rob. "I replaced that with a diesel. I also got rid of the side-venting exhaust and added a copper stack."

To increase headroom in the main saloon, Rob raised one section of the cabin roof and added a skylight fitted with beveled glass. Entering through the aft companionway, you immediately feel a sense of comfort and nostalgia. The galley is to either side and leads forward to the main cabin, which has seating both port and starboard and is furnished with a table with plants, antiques, and a music stand. To port, a passageway with utilities, bookshelves, and storage cabinets leads forward to a small unique head that has a Pullman-style sink and the original bronze toilet. Beyond this area is the office-stateroom, including a rolltop desk. Steps lead up to a pilothouse that could only have been designed in the early twentieth century and is still just the way it was then.

As Kathy and I get the tour, the other musicians relax inside the long narrow saloon, spinning yarns and making plans. "We usually rehearse here on the boat. On a warm summer or fall night, I take her out and drop anchor in one of the coves up around Maple Bay. We sit out there in the aft cockpit. The music off the water and against those rock cliffs is unbelievable—better than a concert hall."

Rob shows me the tiny forepeak cabin that was his daughter's when she was growing up. Now married with a family of her own, she has returned to the island and established a local medical practice.

"Her son will inherit this boat someday," says Rob. "I'll teach him about the water and to enjoy boating, the way my father taught me. When I get too old to look after the boat, it will become his. He can bring me down now and then and take me out for a Sunday cruise."

Rob shows us a copy of an amusing letter from Henry Hoffar, founder of the Hoffar-Beeching shipyard, that describes the day he cut the boat in half back in 1924. It's time to leave, but it's difficult to go—*Cleodoxa* is so comfortable, so enticing, and the musicians are still telling tales. Her narrow hull rolls gently as the wake slaps against the dock.

Columbia

Bill McKechnie

Victoria, British Columbia

*I*n Margaret Craven's classic novel, *I Heard the Owl Call My Name*, the protagonist is a young vicar who sets out from Alert Bay along the rugged British Columbia coastline to a remote native village called Kingcome. There, his life becomes analogous to the journey of the "swimmer"—the name given the salmon by the Kwagiutl people. It is a sorrowful story about months of isolation and dark winter skies. It's also about the vanishing customs, art, and culture of the "salmon people," whose only link to the rest of civilization is a few small wooden boats that became known as "God's Little Ships." For many decades, they were owned and operated by the Anglican Church as part of its Columbia Coast Mission fleet. Several of the boats still survive under private ownership, loosely scattered around the Pacific Northwest.

A thoughtful mission boat owner sent me a video copy of a black-and-white film produced by the Canadian government in the 1950s, entitled *Mission Ships*. Filmed in the village of Kingcome, the setting for Craven's novel, it documents the remote destinations, logging camps, and Indian villages regularly visited by *Columbia*, one of the mission ships. Nowadays the *Columbia* is used to ferry kayakers along the British Columbia coastline during the summer.

Columbia began her life in 1956 as a combination hospital, chapel, dental office, and floating movie theater. Built specifically for the Columbia Coast Mission fleet, she was one of "God's Little Ships" that served the remote camps and villages dotting 20,000 square miles of jagged British Columbia coastline. The task was simple: minister to the medical, dental, and spiritual needs of people at logging camps, native villages, and fishing camps 365 days a year in every type of weather and sea conditions.

"I was actually present at her launching," says current owner, Bill McKechnie. "When I was fifteen, I worked as a volunteer one

summer with the Columbia Coast Mission. That was back in 1956, and all of us got invited to watch the *Columbia* slide down the ways the day she was christened."

Bill notes with amusement that he never saw the boat again until thirty years later, when she came up for sale in 1986. "At the time, I was looking for a good-sized boat to restore," says Bill. "The *Columbia* was in very poor condition. She had deteriorated badly and was being used as a forest-service bunkhouse for seasonal workers."

Bill offered to buy her, but his bid was unsuccessful; a year and a half later, she was back on the market. "I had looked long and hard for a boat like her, with no success, so when my second chance came around, I didn't hesitate or quibble about the price."

This was the beginning of a six-year restoration project that

Columbia

YEAR:	1956
DESIGNER:	Robert Allen Sr.
BUILDER:	Star Shipyards, New Westminster, British Columbia
LENGTH:	67 feet
BEAM:	16 feet, 5 inches
DRAFT:	6 feet, 5 inches
ORIGINAL POWER:	Gardner 8L3, diesel (900 rpm)
CURRENT POWER:	Same
CONSTRUCTION:	First-growth Douglas cedar over oak frames (partly sheathed in gumwood), yellow-cedar freeboard, fir decks, marine-ply house
HOME PORT:	Victoria, British Columbia

has culminated in the boat the *Columbia* is today. "My system was to work on one section of the boat at a time, between the months of January and May. Then I would spend the summer and fall cruising before starting on the next section in January again."

Bill's system has clearly paid off, transforming what had once been a flophouse into one of the most elegantly decorated and refurbished historic vessels on the West Coast. From the gleaming exterior paint and brightwork to her immaculate engine room, *Columbia* is a tribute to one man's perseverance and reverence for historical and cultural treasures. The boat is filled with paintings, artifacts, and remembrances of her past and the places she served.

"Parts of the chapel are still visible," notes Bill. "When I bought her, she'd been through some rather poor modifications, but I've tried to correct those and stay in keeping with the period when she was built."

Many wooden boats have followed a similar path of tears, and the *Columbia* is no exception. They were built for a specific purpose and faithfully served that purpose for decades, often under arduous conditions, until they became obsolete by virtue of progress. Float planes and high-speed inflatables, for example, replaced the old mission ships. When no longer needed, the old boats were discarded and allowed to sit and rot, their upkeep no longer economically sound.

"I tried to keep the restoration true to her era but, at the same time, incorporate the functionality a boat like this would have today," Bill says.

This approach produced excellent results. *Columbia*'s large covered aft deck is ideal for lounging, sightseeing, and photographing the fjords and glaciers of the Pacific Northwest. Her huge saloon has full-sized windows all around, and is warmly enhanced by a large brass diesel stove. The galley is modern, attractive, and spacious enough for two people to work comfortably. *Columbia*'s pilothouse is roomy, resplendent in both antiques and modern navigation instruments, and affords a marvelous view from behind the large front-to-side windows.

Below decks, the staterooms are modest, comfortable, and in perfect keeping with *Columbia*'s character and history. The joinery work is of the finest quality, and the furnishings and art-

work throughout honor the people and places she spent most of her life serving.

"We used the boat for pleasure until 1992," says Bill. "Then I started taking kayakers with me up through the Inside Passage and dropping them off. That eventually evolved into a full-time summer business."

Today, the *Columbia* plies the same waters for which she was originally designed, still calling on the same ports and meandering through the same inlets. Her configuration is exactly as shown in the government film made in the 1950s, and she's still powered by the same Gardner diesel. *Columbia* is still a mother ship, although now under circumstances of enjoyment rather than heartache.

Cygnus II

DAVID AND RUTH GILLESPIE

New York City, New York

For some people, the experience of seeing a classic wooden yacht is limited to watching the opening scenes of *The Great Gatsby*. For others, it may be plowing past one in their fiberglass powerboats—leaving the old varnished girl rolling in their wake. A lucky few may have the opportunity to stand next to a classic at a wooden boat show or rendezvous, perhaps fortunate enough to be invited aboard. But even those who experience a restored or original classic firsthand are often unaware of the staggering amount of time, effort, resources, and thought invested in the beauty they are appreciating. *Cygnus II* is a perfect case in point.

Built in 1930 for Clifford M. Swan, a White Plains, New York, acoustical engineer, *Cygnus II* filled his desire for a larger boat more suited for long-range cruising than his 38-foot Dawn cruiser *(Cygnus I)*. In 1929, Swan commissioned architect Louis L. Kromholz to design a new boat to be named *Cygnus II*. (Cygnus—Latin for *swan*—is a northern constellation in the Milky Way, thought by ancient astronomers to be shaped like a beautiful swan.)

Considering the state of the economy after the stock market crash—Kromholz's drawings for *Cygnus II* were dated September 1929—it is a wonder she was ever built. Nevertheless, she was launched in late 1930 by the Jakobson & Peterson yard in Brooklyn.

According to her current owners, David and Ruth Gillespie, Swan enjoyed *Cygnus II* for the next decade, but with the advent of World War II, she was commandeered by the military, and then Swan died in 1942. After the war, *Cygnus II* was purchased by Mrs. John O'Brien of Detroit, Michigan. She moved the boat to her summer home in Seal Harbor, Maine, and renamed it *Gitana*. During Mrs. O'Brien's ownership, the boat was well maintained and could be seen frequently cruising the Maine coast.

The Gillespies tell that the boat reclaimed her original

Cygnus II

YEAR:	1930
DESIGNER:	Louis L. Kromholz
BUILDER:	Jakobson & Peterson, Brooklyn, New York
LENGTH:	56 feet
BEAM:	13 feet, 6 inches
DRAFT:	4 feet
ORIGINAL POWER:	Twin 6-cylinder Lathrop, gasoline
CURRENT POWER:	Twin 4-cylinder Yanmar, diesel
CONSTRUCTION:	Carvel-planked cedar over steam-bent oak ribs, mahogany house, spruce decks
HOME PORT:	New York City, New York

name in 1955 under the ownership of J. D. Smith, of Southwest Harbor, Maine, who lived aboard. In 1988, *Cygnus II* was again sold as a liveaboard to a Rhode Island couple, and at that time four typewritten pages of repairs were required before she could be safely towed to Jamestown. From there, she was eventually towed to Mystic, Connecticut.

The long periods of neglect are completely invisible today. In fact, no one who boards *Cygnus II* would ever suspect she once required the degree of restoration she has undergone since the current owners purchased her in 1997.

"It was July 1997, and we were having a great time at the Mystic Seaport Antique and Classic Boat Rendezvous in our Dawn 45," says David. "Great boats and old friends. Ruth was off shopping in the museum store, so I walked into town to get an ice cream cone. And that's when I saw her for the first time."

David admits that the boat he saw that morning is a far cry from the boat he now owns; nonetheless, he was able to envision the metamorphosis that would eventually take place. She was tied up at an old dock, and he could just glimpse the for-sale sign; even from that distance, he could see she had beautiful lines.

"As I got closer," David says, "I began to see other things. What looked like mahogany brightwork was actually peeling brown paint. Toerails were missing. The transom had rot. Decks were fiberglassed."

Unlike many older boats David had seen over the years, *Cygnus II* seemed to have retained most of her original hardware —especially pieces that are now nearly impossible to find. No one had added a flybridge or any other awful changes. Her hull seemed fair and had not lost shape, and—best of all, according to David—she had a perfect layout and lots of headroom.

When you step aboard *Cygnus II*, you can appreciate the kind of cruising comfort that Clifford Swan had in mind when the boat was designed in 1929. His requirements were for large, open decks with built-in seating. Aft is a spacious cabin with a double berth and a daybed. The large head has a 4-foot tub-shower. The wheelhouse is located over the engine room and has two seats for guests. Originally, it was open-sided, but sliding doors were added later to provide full enclosure in bad weather. Forward is a large dining saloon fitted with a built-in settee, yacht table, a dish pantry, and a panel bed for guests. To port there is a small day head, and located forward is a full-width galley that still has the original Shipmate gas stove. Forward of the galley are crew quarters for two and an additional head.

The ensuing restoration took the Gillespies three years and an untold number of hours. David and Ruth did most of the work, enlisting the help of the yard for larger items such as the new flattop and aft decks. Working with the original plans and photographs from the Mystic Seaport Ship's Plans and the Rosenfeld Photograph Collections, the Gillespies set out to return *Cygnus II* to her original state of grace. According to David, replacement items included the flattop aft-deck covering, which had been rebuilt with unsupported plywood. The aft and side decks were severely deteriorated, as were the forward trunk cabintop and sides. Because the main saloon had been gutted, it had to be rebuilt to original specifications; the day head was eventually converted to a laundry.

Every system in the boat was replaced. Every inch of wiring was removed and replaced, and original light fixtures were rebuilt to ensure safety. All plumbing was removed and replaced to the water tank, which was then removed and repaired. In the engine room, a new generator and two new diesel engines were in-

stalled, along with other equipment including an inverter, autopilot, and water pumps.

In 1999, *Cygnus II* was relaunched in time for the Mystic Seaport Antique and Classic Boat Rendezvous. Even in her unfinished state, she earned a special citation for "best ongoing restoration." And by the time of the 2000 show, she was restored enough to take "best powerboat" in her class.

From a distance or even close up, at best we can only see these boats on the surface. Their varnished mahogany and gleaming brass jump out at us, making us envy their owners, but it is difficult to fathom what it takes to revive these marvelous old wooden entities. Only after seeing the before and after photographs, or learning something of their history, can we begin to appreciate the effort, money, and dedication required for their rebirth.

Duchess

JACK LEONARD

Lyme, Connecticut

Duchess, a well-known boat on the Connecticut River, has for many years been the lead boat at the Antique and Classic Boat Rendez-vous at Mystic Seaport, Connecticut. Each year, as thousands of people line the banks to watch, a parade of classic yachts travels down the Mystic River, under the drawbridge, through the quaint town of Mystic, and out to Long Island Sound and back. In addition to this honor, *Duchess* has earned numerous awards, including Best Power, 40-foot and under, 1995; Special Citation for Long-Standing Support, 1988; Special Award, 1981; and Certificate of Excellence by the Yachting Committee of the Mystic Seaport Museum, 1989, for her outstanding design, construction, and history.

"We had a summer cottage on a large lake, and my dad acquainted me with boating when I was very young," says owner Jack Leonard.

Jack soon became an avid sailor, boating in places like Buzzard's Bay, Massachusetts. Shortly after graduation from college in 1938, he began working on submarines for a diesel engine and submarine company in Groton, Connecticut, and remained there for forty-four years.

"In 1962, I moved to Lyme, Connecticut. There is a famous and beautiful anchorage there called Hamburg Cove, with two marinas. Berthing there was a beautiful custom motor yacht named *Stella Maris*."

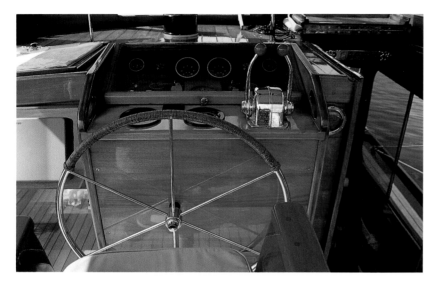

Jack explains that, as time went on, he became more infatuated with both the boat and the small marina where it was moored. When the boat came up for sale, Jack felt the price was too high, and someone else bought the boat of his dreams.

"In 1972, the *Stella Maris* came up for sale again," says Jack. "This time, they wanted even more money than before, but I bought her without hesitation. A few years later, the yard—which was nearly defunct by then—came on the market and I bought it, too."

Stella Maris, which Jack renamed *Duchess* after his wife's nickname, had been allowed to deteriorate over the years. He and his son John embarked on a total restoration.

"Her original Chrysler Crowns, which had given her a top speed of 13 knots, had been replaced by Chrysler eight-cylinders. These were the engines in the boat when I bought her."

According to Jack, the larger Chrysler engines were raw-water cooled, and eventually they corroded. He replaced them with the Ford Lehmans, along with new instrumentation and operating controls. Drive shafts were realigned and new bearings were installed. All electrical systems were completely replaced and new electrical panels installed. Eventually, all new electronic navigation was added, as well as new heads and plumbing, tanks, and exhaust systems. Both the interior and exterior were completely wooded and refinished. The original decks were removed and replaced with teak.

The view *Duchess* presents from a distance belies her layout. The traditional forward cabin has two bunks with a hanging locker and storage under the bottom bunk. However, the rest of the layout includes a second sleeping cabin with one bunk, storage under the bottom bunk, a hanging locker, and an enclosed head; and the third cabin, which is raised, functions as a galley-saloon, with a large couch that pulls out to a double berth. There is an outside steering station under canvas and an aft cabin, accessible by a hatch, which has a double bunk, dresser, head, and clothes locker.

Jack uses *Duchess* primarily as a family cruiser, plying virtually all the waters of Eastern Long Island to Nantucket, Martha's Vineyard, Cutty Hunk, Narragansett Bay, and Shelter Island.

"In 1995, we went on a cruise with four other classics," Jack says, "traveling down to New York City; up the Hudson to Albany; through the Erie Canal to Oswego, New York; across Lake Ontario and into Canada; then up the Rideau Canal system to Ottawa; then down to the St. Lawrence; and eventually, back down to Albany and our home port. The trip covered more than 1,700 miles and traversed 101 locks."

The exterior brightwork on *Duchess* is amazing. Her natural decks, gleaming chrome hardware, and varnished trunk cabins testify to decades of care and hard work. Jack notes that his son John did much of the restoration on this beautiful 1950s vintage cruiser, and he intends to carry on the tradition for years to come.

Duchess

YEAR:	1950
DESIGNER:	Unknown
BUILDER:	Sound Marine Construction, Long Island, New York
LENGTH:	40 feet
BEAM:	13 feet
DRAFT:	3 feet
ORIGINAL POWER:	Twin Chrysler Crowns
CURRENT POWER:	Twin 6-cylinder Ford Lehman, gasoline
CONSTRUCTION:	Honduras-mahogany planks over white-oak frames, mahogany superstructure
HOME PORT:	Lyme, Connecticut

Eslo

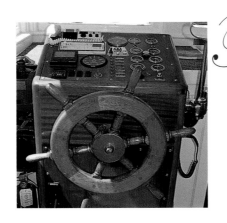

TOM AND NANCY CLOTHIER

San Francisco, California

Tom Clothier says that his life consists of four equally important parts: his family, his job, his boat, and his game of golf. "It seemed there was never enough time to satisfy each, so I retired from my job."

Since retirement, he happily spends most of his time on the care and maintenance of *Eslo*, a one-design handmade raised-deck cruiser built in 1940 by Lowell A. Netherland, of Brisbane, California. Netherland used the boat for several decades in the northern California coastal waters, the San Francisco Bay, and the Sacramento and San Joaquin Deltas. In 1968, *Eslo* was sold to Edward Galloway, a San Francisco writer who lived aboard until his death in 1980. The boat sat neglected until 1992, when the Clothiers bought her.

Eslo was original in every way when they found her, yet time had taken its toll. "Between 1992 and 1998, I invested over three thousand hours in the boat, replacing the entire electrical system, decking, cabinetry, cabin soles, water tanks, interior staircases, and mahogany trim."

Tom adds that the hull, which is 1½ inches of Port Orford cedar over 3-inch sawn-oak frames, was taken to bare wood, routed, and recaulked. *Eslo*'s original handrails were ½-inch steel pipe, which he replaced with mahogany.

"I installed forty-seven new stanchions, wrapped in twine and coated with high-build epoxy barrier and topside enamel. Then I cut the rails from Honduras mahogany planks. I also added a cockpit cover—built to two thirds the scale of the pilothouse—which increased our usable space substantially."

The immediate charm of this boat is in her attractive and roomy interior, which is bright and naturally lit by the large portlights both forward and aft. In addition, her interior has been decorated with taste and attention to detail, much like a sophisticated San Francisco apartment. The colorful wallpaper, curtains, pictures, brightly painted storage cabinets, upholstery, and furnishings are a welcome change from the traditional

varnished mahogany or teak interiors. *Eslo*'s forward cabin, with bunks both port and starboard, is exceptionally roomy with large hanging lockers located just before the pilothouse entry. The house is bright, with seating behind the steering station. The entry to the galley-main saloon is to starboard. A quaint dinette is located to port as you step down, and the rest of the room is large, open, and bright. The 13-foot beam makes this boat a most comfortable and functional classic design.

In 1999, Tom repowered *Eslo* with a Detroit 671-N; the original engine was a Gray Marine 671 that ran well and appeared to have never been touched, but he wanted the peace of mind of the Detroit. "I'm particularly proud of *Eslo* because 99 percent of the labor involved in her restoration was just me. The only outside help I enlisted was a crane operator for the installation of the Detroit diesel."

Tom and Nancy intend to take their boat on a trip to the Pacific Northwest in 2002. Her lovely, roomy, and airy interior will make the extended cruise a pleasure.

Eslo	
YEAR:	1940
DESIGNER:	Lowell A. Netherland, Brisbane, California
BUILDER:	Lowell A. Netherland, Brisbane, California
LENGTH:	47 feet
BEAM:	13 feet
DRAFT:	4 feet, 10 inches
ORIGINAL POWER:	Gray Marine 671
CURRENT POWER:	Detroit 671-N
CONSTRUCTION:	Port Orford cedar over oak frames
HOME PORT:	San Francisco, California

Euphemia II

MIKE AND PEGGY O'BRIEN

Vancouver, British Columbia

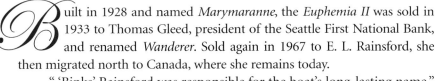

uilt in 1928 and named *Marymaranne*, the *Euphemia II* was sold in 1933 to Thomas Gleed, president of the Seattle First National Bank, and renamed *Wanderer*. Sold again in 1967 to E. L. Rainsford, she then migrated north to Canada, where she remains today.

" 'Binks' Rainsford was responsible for the boat's long-lasting name," says current owner Mike O'Brien. "Mr. Rainsford's family had a tradition of naming the first daughter in each generation *Euphemia* (French for "good sounding"). However, Mrs. Rainsford flatly refused to call her daughter Euphemia, so Rainsford applied it to his boat."

Rainsford owned the boat until 1967, when he sold it to Floyd Stanley of Maple Bay, British Columbia. Stanley, a local surgeon in Duncan, owned the boat until his death in 1998.

"We first saw *Euphemia II* back in the summer of 1974," recalls Mike, "and it was long-term love at first sight." Based on their admiration for the boat, Mike and his wife Peggy eventually became friends with "Doc" Stanley, and spent many summers cruising together while aboard their own boat, the *Nomad I.* As Doc grew older, though, it became increasingly more difficult for him to maintain his boat.

"We approached him several times about selling the boat, but Doc

would never consider it. He never wanted to let his boat go. *Euphemia II* meant the world to him, and he and his wife cruised the boat extensively each summer."

When Floyd passed away in 1998, his wife contacted the O'Briens and told them that Doc wanted them to have the boat. "We weren't in the market for a boat then," says Mike. "We had our own classic cruiser, the *Haida Princess*, that we had restored, but we had no choice. We couldn't allow *Euphemia II* to be sold to someone else."

Entirely original and showing her age from years of minimal maintenance, *Euphemia II* underwent a transformation in the hands of the O'Briens. Their admiration of and early dream of one day owning her are perhaps at the core of the beautiful restoration they achieved.

Planked with Port Orford cedar, Mike notes, the boat had always been sound, and they began cruising her the first week they owned her. They gradually began addressing such tasks as removing old wallpaper, wiring, plumbing, and bubbled paint and

varnish; and replacing floors, upholstery, and exterior canvas, as well as adding lovely interior furnishings and nautical antiques.

Yachts built by the Schertzer Boat Works of Seattle, Washington, have an unmistakable signature design: the camber overall, the forward look of the pilothouse, and the plumb bows make them easily recognizable at any gathering of classics. Although there is only a handful left (*Euphemia II*, *Kiyi*, *Shearwater*, *Rum Runner*, *Hanna*, and perhaps a few others), Schertzer boats attract a subculture among classic yacht enthusiasts (like Avanti cars or Epiphone guitars) and are respected for their interior comfort and exceptionally smooth ride.

"*Euphemia* has a safe, sure feeling underway," says Mike, "more so than any boat I've ever cruised. And her interior layout is perfect—whether it's just the two of us or we're having family or friends aboard. She's spacious and comfortable."

Euphemia II's comfort begins forward with a large sleeping cabin that includes a full head in the forepeak, hanging lockers, plenty of storage, and ample headroom. The pilothouse is almost saloon-sized, with spacious seating for four or even six while underway or at anchor. The galley, abaft the wheelhouse and to port, has an L-shaped sink and countertop and is opposite the original

Euphemia II

YEAR:	1928
DESIGNER:	Unknown
BUILDER:	Schertzer Boat Works, Seattle, Washington
LENGTH:	50 feet
BEAM:	10 feet, 7 inches
DRAFT:	4 feet, 6 inches
ORIGINAL POWER:	6-cylinder Sterling, gasoline
CURRENT POWER:	Volvo 50 TMD
CONSTRUCTION:	Port Orford cedar on oak frames
HOME PORT:	Vancouver, British Columbia

refrigerator and an enclosed head. The spacious main saloon is open, with excellent headroom and comfortable settee-bunks to each side with a large dining table between. Especially noteworthy in this area are the oversized bronze portlights, the tasteful new upholstery, and the gorgeous new flooring Mike installed. The aft companionway leads up to a covered cockpit furnished with attractive wicker chairs, reminiscent of the Roaring Twenties.

Euphemia II exemplifies the magical power and influence these floating dreams have over those of us who admire them. We are reluctant to let them go, even when we are no longer able to maintain them. The allure can begin with an infatuation before we ever own one, and continues with the willingness to restore its glory when given the chance to stand our watch; the allure is never-ending.

Forest Surveyor

MARK AND JULIE DAVISCOURT

Seattle, Washington

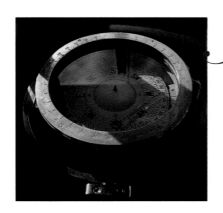

I am standing on the south side of Seattle's ship canal, just above the Hiram M. Chittenden locks that connect Lake Union with the Puget Sound. With binoculars, I am scanning the north shore, sweeping past the congested marinas, shipyards, and freight docks—hundreds of boats: everything from rusted steel tankers to plastic megayachts to half-submerged daysailers. Eventually, I spot *Forest Surveyor:* her pilothouse perched on top of the main house; her blunt, plumb bow facing the canal. Had I not just been aboard this boat, I doubt that I could have found her from this distance. Through the binoculars, she's just another workboat leaning against the dock in the wind. That strikes me as ironic.

The tip came from a classic yachter who told me about a workboat located in the marina in which his boat was moored, explaining that she was going through a total refit. "Just a plain-Jane workboat," he said, "that is, until you step aboard her."

Industrial elegance, extreme modesty, purposefully phenomenal—I don't know how to describe what we found when we boarded *Forest Surveyor.* She was built during World War II for the Canadian military, serving out the final years of the war as a submarine surveillance boat off

the Aleutian Islands. Designed and massively constructed to military specifications, her hull is double-planked Douglas fir over white-oak frames with a gumwood stem, horn, and caprails, and ice sheathing at the bow. Her original power was a Gray Marine diesel, replaced in 1965 by a Detroit 871—which is probably the most logical place to start the description.

Forest Surveyor is every boater's dream: a walk-in engine room that is as clean as a church with well-lit workbenches, generous tool storage, and all critical systems—especially fuel filters and breaker panels—within easy reach. The engine room in Forest Surveyor exceeds the dreams—these features are not only expertly installed, they are also attractive and simple: the stainless steel floors, walkaround 871 diesel, industrial-strength Racors and fire-protection systems, breaker panels mounted just above the workbenches—all comprise a captain's ideal.

Forest Surveyor

YEAR:	1944
DESIGNER:	Unknown
BUILDER:	A. C. Benson, Vancouver, British Columbia
LENGTH:	60 feet
BEAM:	16 feet
DRAFT:	8 feet, 6 inches
ORIGINAL POWER:	Gray Marine, diesel
CURRENT POWER:	Detroit 871, diesel
CONSTRUCTION:	Double-planked Douglas fir over white-oak frames
HOME PORT:	Seattle, Washington

"We began with a naval architect named Tom Henderson," her owner explains. "It was on his recommendation that we decided to start by totally gutting the boat."

"Gutting" is evident in some ways, not in others. Leaving the engine room forward, you enter the master stateroom in the forecastle area—clearly, a conversion tactic. The mahogany joinery work is exquisite, the lighting is almost perfect, and the general comfort is first rate—all cradled by the original massively

laid planking and overhead deck beams. To port, just before the ladder leading to the main house, is a head with a full shower.

Climbing the ladder, you are amazed at the size, elegance, and workboat simplicity of the galley—it seems almost an extension of the engine room. Every inch has been well thought out, magnificently executed, and in keeping with the concept of a military boat built during World War II.

"She was originally designed and built to carry His Majesty's Troops," the owner explains. "Nothing in the way of materials or craftsmanship was spared back then. We decided from the start to honor that tradition."

They did. Each component—from the circular dinette forward to the immense stainless steel cooking station starboard, to the sinks and cupboards port—is both spectacular and in harmony with the character and integrity of this kind of boat (that is, there is no glitz).

Abaft the galley is a large saloon, tastefully accented by tugboat art on the walls, Native American artifacts, and beautiful handcrafted furniture and joinery work. A door leads to the portside outer decks, and a stairwell just abaft the galley descends to the lower staterooms. The aft staterooms are identical in design, and are both comfortable and cozy. It's down here that the extreme stoutness of this boat is most evident: the overhead deck beams, supported by massive knees, are detailed to perfection. Through her bronze portlights, you realize how close the waterline is and how far below it you are standing. *Forest Surveyor* draws 8½ feet.

The pilothouse is accessed only by outside ladders. It's quite small but comfortable, with dual leather captain's chairs, a long seat-bunk conversion behind the chairs, and many electronic navigational aids. The height of this perch and the forward position of the house become apparent when you stand at the wheel and gaze down at the bow, which is otherwise out of sight. The 360-degree visibility from the pilothouse is a distinct advantage.

"After the war, she was operated by the Canadian Forest Service, from 1946 until 1984," her owner explains. Mainly a timber-survey boat, *Forest Surveyor* lived up to her name, surveying the Queen Charlottes off the coast of British Columbia, Vancouver Island, and from Prince Rupert to Ocean Falls. During this period, she served as a towboat and conducted coastal mapping. In 1985, she was put up for sealed bid and was purchased by Peter Brown, who was a full-time liveaboard and used her as a salvage and charter-fishing boat. In 1999, he sold her to the current owner.

"I knew what I wanted in a boat," her owner explains. "I grew up on fishing vessels on the Columbia River in Washington. I wanted a stout, government-built boat with a deep hull and a plumb bow for extended cruising in remote open waters. That's what *Forest Surveyor* was originally designed for."

And it's what she is being used for again—only days after her refit was completed, *Forest Surveyor* left for an extended cruise circumnavigating Vancouver Island where, among other hardships, she encountered full-gale conditions.

"The boat performed perfectly," says her owner. "There was never a moment when we felt unsafe."

He adds that this performance results from the commitment of the people who worked on the restoration. "They understood they were restoring something very significant," he says. "We took the boat to places like Bakketun and Thomas in Seattle, Protrac Systems, and Fishing Vessel Owners, located at Fisherman's Terminal. These are truly some of the last great traditional yards left that deal in heavy workboat and fishing-boat conversions."

These conversions will ultimately produce tomorrow's classic yachts. Most of the surviving wooden pleasure yachts have already been found and been brought back to life. Many of

the marvelous wooden workboats, tugboats, and fishing boats have been lost, but hundreds—like *Forest Surveyor*—still wait to be rediscovered.

I study the boats again across the canal through my binoculars. Perhaps it's because I've photographed and written about so many boats that have spent their long lives pampered with covered moorage and annual sheathings of varnish that I have a special place in my heart for the simple working boats of the world. Where they have gone and what they have done, most of us can only imagine, and they have always come home safely. When owners expend the time and money to give these boats another century of life, it is an endeavor of true merit and foresight—and it must be a lot of fun.

Gwendoline

CURT AND MARSHA ERICKSON

Tacoma, Washington

A common notion among wooden boat owners, to which I frequently subscribe myself, is that "it's all about the boats." But it's more than that: it's about how they affect us, how they shape our lives, and how we often return to them as we would to the important places in our lives. *Gwendoline* is an example in point.

According to Curt Erickson, *Gwendoline* (which is the boat's original name) was commissioned in 1932 by Hugh Baker and named after his wife. The builder, twenty-one-year-old Dick Taylor, was an unemployed shipwright who, like dozens of others during the Great Depression, was looking for anything to help him survive.

"His father and his uncle worked at the Lake Washington Shipyard in Seattle," Curt explained. One day a man walked into the yard looking for an out-of-work shipwright to build a small pleasure yacht on the cheap. Taylor volunteered, and was contracted at 75 cents an hour. Two years later, *Gwendoline* slipped down the greased rails into Lake Washington.

"Her new owners cruised the boat every summer during the 1930s, sometimes as far north as Alaska," Curt says. "It was their dream come true." Curt reminds us that this was long before modern electronics, radars,

Gwendoline

YEAR:	1932
DESIGNER:	Helmut Schmidt
BUILDER:	Dick Taylor, Seattle, Washington
LENGTH:	32 feet
BEAM:	9 feet
DRAFT:	3 feet, 6 inches
ORIGINAL POWER:	4-cylinder Palmer, gasoline
CURRENT POWER:	V-6 Chevy Crusader Vortex
CONSTRUCTION:	Alaska yellow cedar over oak frames, teak house
HOME PORT:	Tacoma, Washington

VHF radios, and electronic depth-sounders. "The compass was really the only navigational aid available back then on boats that size. Cruising from Puget Sound to Alaska in a little 32-foot boat with just a compass was something."

After Mrs. Baker passed away in 1941, her husband stopped using the boat. "I guess he couldn't bear to use the boat after his wife passed away," says Curt. "It was too much a part of both of them. He never resumed cruising."

After 1942, *Gwendoline* went through ten owners before Curt and Marsha eventually found her in 1995. "We've had six of the previous owners on board. Almost every one had a significant impact on the boat's survival over the decades."

None of the former owners altered the original design of the boat, and they all completed their part of the restoration competently and professionally—rare in boats of this vintage.

"The previous owner had put a lot of time and money into restoring the boat," Curt says. "He sold her once, but claimed the buyer didn't take care of her very well, so he bought her back." A friend of Curt knew of the boat, and when she came up for sale again, he knew Curt would offer it a good home.

Curt and Marsha are by no means amateur wooden boat enthusiasts. Curt's collection of runabouts and antique race boats includes a restored 1938 Chris Craft triple cockpit, a 1929 Dodge Watercar, and a Disappearing Propeller Boat—not to mention a 1906 racing launch, a fantail launch, two Fairliner torpedoes, a 16-foot Dodge, and a custom-built race boat.

"We went to see *Gwendoline* on our friend's recommendation and immediately fell in love with her," Curt says. "So we invited the owner to our house to see some of our other boats. I guess he was impressed enough to sell."

Since owning *Gwendoline*, Curt has made several improvements. "We completely did the interior, took all surfaces to bare wood, installed new carpets, new wiring—all of that. Marsha

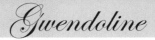

made hand carvings for the cabinet doors and head, and etched some of the windows."

The striking feature about *Gwendoline*—in addition to her magnificent condition—is how bright she is, a result of the large windows in both the pilothouse and the galley area. The traditional layout includes a small V-berth forward, a dinette inside the wheelhouse, a galley abaft via steps to starboard, and two upper single bunks in the aft cabin. The enclosed head is located to port across from the galley, and there is a comfortable cockpit space beyond the trunk cabin. Powered by a V-6 Chevy Crusader, *Gwendoline* has a tight, confident feeling when underway and can be easily maneuvered in tight quarters.

An interesting approach that Curt has taken is to install modern electronics that can be concealed from view when not in use. His years of experience in restoring and rebuilding runabouts and race boats are evident when you examine this boat closely: every inch is perfection. From the major improvements to the artistry that Marsha brings to the restoration process, *Gwendoline* is a boat to be proud of.

Through friends, Curt and Marsha located Dick Taylor, the original builder, whom they invited, along with his wife, aboard for lunch and an afternoon cruise.

"He was eighty-eight at the time. Dick told us that *Gwendoline* was the most important boat he ever built, because it gave him the wherewithal to ask his wife Madeline to marry him. Neither one of them had been aboard her for sixty-six years," Curt says, "but he remembered every inch of the boat. He was amazed at the condition she's in today. Having them aboard was one of the most precious experiences of our lives, that's for sure."

Halcyon

SAM AND PAM FRY

Friday Harbor, Washington

It's a hazy Sunday morning in late summer. Wildfires are burning in the Washington Cascades and a dense white fog is parked in the Rosario Strait west of Anacortes. I know from experience that the breeze will push the haze back against the Cascades, and that by ten in the morning, the sun will dissipate the fog as it burns off to a beautiful blue-sky day.

I'm on my way to Shipyard Cove on San Juan Island to finish shooting *Halcyon*. I have one of the best jobs in the world, traveling to marinas and unique ports like Sidney, British Columbia; Newport, Rhode Island; and Monterey, California. I'm invited aboard and taken out on cruises on some of the loveliest classic wooden yachts afloat. While writing about and photographing classics, I've made lasting friendships with fine folks and have been enraptured by the beauty and mystique of classic wooden boats. Today will be no exception.

I first saw *Halcyon* at Maple Bay Marina on the east coast of Vancouver Island during the spring wooden boat festival. Destroyed by a fire and found by the current owner in neglected condition, she's now a perfectly restored and rebuilt fishing boat.

"I saw her listing about 20 degrees at a dock on Orcas Island," Sam Fry remembers. "The wheelhouse and trunk cabin had been totally destroyed

and all you could see forward was total blackness. The forward decks had been burned through, as well. But I loved the hourglass stern and the shear of the decks, plus that signature Bill Garden flair to the bow."

A shipwright by trade, Sam eventually located the owner and worked out a series of deals that involved satisfying various liens against the boat. "It took about six months, but she was finally mine," Sam recalls, smiling about the messy ordeal. He then embarked on a decade-long restoration.

Sam was working in a yard where the owner allowed him to keep the boat and work on her in his free time. He was able to maintain the boat's original house and trunk cabin, except for slightly raising the cabin roof for more headroom and lowering the pilothouse floor. "I wanted the boat to still look like a fishing boat from 100 yards away, and I'm happy that she does."

It took a month of hauling away burned debris in his pickup truck before he could even see the engine room. It was there that Sam discovered what he refers to as "the great yellow

Halcyon

YEAR:	1948
DESIGNER:	William Garden
BUILDER:	Wes and Norm Anderson
	Phinney Bay, Washington
LENGTH:	34 feet, 6 inches (LOA 40 feet)
BEAM:	10 feet, 6 inches
DRAFT:	5 feet, 5 inches
ORIGINAL POWER:	Unknown make, gasoline
CURRENT POWER:	1936 Cat D4400
CONSTRUCTION:	Carvel-planked fir on oak
HOME PORT:	Friday Harbor, Washington

monster": a 1936 Cat with virtually no hours, that had been installed in 1955. After the wheelhouse, trunk cabin, and decks were removed, Sam began steam-blasting the hull to remove char from the wood and clean up the odors.

Perhaps only an experienced shipwright would tackle such a task, but the effort has produced a remarkably comfortable and attractive boat. The forward cabin, which has a spacious V-berth under the massive windlass, is entered via short steps to starboard. Included is a comfortable seating and dressing area abaft the bunk. The pilothouse is a two-seater at best, with the steering station to port and a fold-down chart table to starboard. Step outside to enter the trunk cabin through a gorgeous teak hatch, then descend to an attractive, compact, and comfortable galley-

dinette-saloon combination. There is a small head to port and a large engine room access next to the teak entry ladder.

"When redesigning the aft cabin," Sam says, "it was important to put back the strength that was lost by removing so many deck beams when raising the cabintop to form the trunk cabin."

As an experienced shipwright, Sam was able to maintain or increase the structural integrity of the boat while achieving the yacht-like joinery of beautiful woods. His design and workmanship produced a special blend of structural stoutness and handcrafted elegance—a talent to be envied by wooden boat owners.

Kathy and I have just enjoyed a relaxed lunch with Pam and Sam. Sitting inside that marvelous boat, it was difficult to believe the restoration story he told us. Even more amazing is the fact that everything was handmade by this talented man. Classic yachts become icons of antiquity; we view them as we might famous paintings in a museum. *Halcyon* and her owners exemplify that process.

Linmar

DAVE OLSON

Oakland, California

The *Linmar* is an affront to the very essence of the Fordian concept of mass production and the postwar sensibilities that both accepted and propagated everything from Levittown to McDonald's. She is special: elegant, private, and perhaps elitist, yet truly a 1930s product of New York City's wealth, sophistication, and art deco extravagance. The decks and spacious aft lounge recall *Gatsby* at every glance: the antique wooden radios, the 1930s lighting fixtures, and the carved bedstead in the main stateroom look just the way Jazz-age music still sounds.

"I missed the boat in 1995," says current owner, Dave Olson. "Then found her for sale again up in Seattle in 1998."

Linmar was built in 1933 by the New York Yacht, Launch & Engine Company, located in Morris Heights on the Harlem River across from Manhattan. At that time, her design was referred to as a *houseboat*. She was constructed for Howard Marlin of New London, Connecticut, whose family business was Marlin Arms, a famous rifle-manufacturing company. The Marlin family used *Linmar* primarily as an intracoastal cruiser until the late 1930s, when the boat was moved to Canada.

"We have very little information about her history then," says Dave. "However, we know that during the late 1940s, she returned to the United

States, went through several owners, and wound up in Florida, where she was renamed *Seaplay*."

In 1964, a Dr. Wayne Bush purchased the boat and brought her to the San Francisco Bay area; he is largely credited with saving the boat. During his tenure as *Linmar*'s steward—which lasted well into the 1990s—Dr. Bush saw considerable work done to her hull, replacing a number of planks.

In 1995, *Linmar* left the Bay area, briefly relocating to Seattle, Washington, where she was used as a charter vessel to ply the coastlines of Washington, British Columbia, and Alaska. In 1998, she was purchased by the Olson family and brought back to her familiar home waters of the San Francisco Bay Area.

Part of the unique attraction of *Linmar*'s design is the matter of space. Although by nature boats have "space" in moderation, at best, there is a sense of shoulder room when moving about *Linmar*. Her aft deck, enclosed by glass, is suitable for modest social events and is ideal for lounging or strolling while

YEAR:	1933
DESIGNER:	Unknown
BUILDER:	New York Yacht, Launch & Engine Company, Morris Heights, New York
LENGTH:	78 feet
BEAM:	18 feet, 6 inches
DRAFT:	6 feet
ORIGINAL POWER:	Twin Winton, diesel
CURRENT POWER:	Twin GMC 6-110, diesel
CONSTRUCTION:	Double-planked Port Orford cedar hull, teak superstructure and decks
HOME PORT:	Oakland, California

underway or at anchor. This delightful space becomes part of the main saloon by means of French doors, doubling the size of the room. The sense of space in her main saloon is enhanced by the oversized windows, both port and starboard.

Forward and beyond the pilothouse is an elegant formal dining room: the teak joinery work, nickel furnishings and lighting, framed artwork, remarkable nickel-plated portlights, and large windows port and starboard are signature features of the NYYL&E design—a concept that few vintage yachts achieve.

Forward and below is the galley, crew quarters, and access to the engine room. The guest and master cabins are accessed via a stairwell located in the main saloon. The huge master cabin is forward, followed by two single and two double cabins. Each of the two heads has a cast-iron bathtub.

It is fortunate that *Linmar* was one of the boats extensively photographed in the 1930s by Rosenfeld, whose work is now housed in the Mystic Seaport Museum in Connecticut. "We've been able to use these historic photos to try and restore the boat to her exact design and splendor," says Dave. "We were very fortunate to have such a resource."

Originally powered by twin Winton diesels, which were replaced during the 1950s with twin GMC 6-110 diesels, *Linmar* is double-planked with Port Orford cedar. Her superstructure is constructed of teak with teak decks. She carries double launches topside and has covered outer decks—both port and starboard—leading forward and aft.

Linmar's typical cruising waters are between San Francisco and Monterey Bay, but Dave's future plans include the Pacific Northwest, Alaska, and southern California waters.

Lorelei

STEVE AND MARY JANE SHELDON

Olympia, Washington

lthough commonly thought of as the major production-yacht builder of the 1960s and 1970s, Chris Craft, of Algonac, Michigan, was building beautiful wooden pleasure boats well before World War II. *Lorelei* is an example of the builder's early quality, craftsmanship, design, and standards, which easily match many of the one-of-a-kind boats of that period.

Lorelei's owners, Steve and Mary Jane Sheldon, had previously owned a Chris Craft runabout, but were in the market for a medium-sized fiberglass cruiser with diesel power suitable for long-range summer cruising.

"But then we stumbled on *Lorelei* by accident. We had no intention of buying another wooden boat, but her age, her profile, and that endlessly long foredeck that was a Chris trademark of that period grabbed us—the way wooden boats often do—and a year later we wound up owning her."

After production, the boat was shipped to Florida, where she was used as a sportfisher for ten years. In 1947, she was brought to Tacoma, Washington, by the Robert Hale family and remained at the Tacoma Yacht Club until 1972. Because the Hales used the boat extensively for northwest cruising between Washington and Alaska, they added a flybridge and enclosed the aft cabin, which created a pilothouse in place of the sportfisher steering station.

The current interior gives no indication that the pilothouse was once an open steering station. Hale added a long settee for lounging and passenger viewing while underway, which also pulls out to a double berth. The pilothouse now functions as a comfortable saloon-steering station. A center companionway leads to the area below, with a dinette to starboard and second settee-berth to port. The enclosed head has the original bronze toilet with "Chris Craft" embossed on the bronze handle. Across from the head is *Lorelei*'s original and functional galley with extensive counter and sink space, plus storage above and below. Forward of the galley is a traditional, large V-berth.

Steve notes that although Hale made most of the major modifications to the boat—including repowering in 1961 with the current 430 Chris Craft engine—subsequent owners also greatly improved the boat.

"We bought her from a man named George Leago," Steve says. "He was an auto mechanic who made countless improvements to the boat that, for the most part, are never seen." Those improvements include new water tanks, gasoline tanks, holding tanks, hot water, cabin heat, electronic ignition, and all new belts, wiring, and plumbing.

Since taking ownership five years ago, the Sheldons have performed extensive work on the boat as well. "Our efforts have mainly been cosmetic," Steve notes. Improvements under the Sheldons' watch include rechroming all the exterior hardware, new upholstery and carpets, paint and varnish, and storage cabinets installed under the seating in the aft cabin.

"*Lorelei* has always been kept in excellent condition," Steve adds, "so it was easy to concentrate on her appearance."

Steve and Mary Jane plan to circumnavigate Vancouver Island in *Lorelei*. Their hope is to organize a trip involving one or two other classics. Conditions along the Northwest coast can become quite treacherous, as many boaters quickly learn. Steve notes that, "to take a boat this old on a cruise that extensive requires research on weather patterns, currents, tides."

Lorelei

YEAR:	1937
DESIGNER:	Chris Craft
BUILDER:	Chris Craft, Algonac, Michigan
LENGTH:	36 feet
BEAM:	11 feet
DRAFT:	2 feet, 8 inches
ORIGINAL POWER:	6-cylinder Chris Craft Model MR
CURRENT POWER:	V-8 Chris Craft 430
CONSTRUCTION:	Double-planked mahogany hull, mahogany superstructure
HOME PORT:	Olympia, Washington

Master

SS Master Society

Vancouver, British Columbia

She spent her life towing log booms and barges of wood, coal, and oil. Although the scope of her operations was primarily the waters of British Columbia, she's worked as far south as California and as far north as Alaska. Built in 1922 at the Beach Avenue Shipyard in Vancouver, British Columbia, *Master* was virtually abandoned to looters and neglect by her owners in 1959 at the mouth of the Pitt River.

Built for Captain Herman Thorsen, at a cost believed to be approximately $34,000, she was one of three almost identical wood-hulled tugs built by Arthur Moscrop. According to Doug Shaw, currently an engineer on *Master*, Moscrop was one of the most notable tugboat builders in British Columbia. *Master* is the sole surviving Moscrop tug that remains original in design and is still operating under her original steam power.

"Her expansion steam engine was built in Scotland in 1916 as one of a pair to be installed in a minesweeper," notes Doug. "The minesweeper was never finished, and the engines were sold as war surplus, one going in the *Master* and the other into her sister ship, the *RFM.*"

According to Doug, her first boiler was built in Victoria and then replaced in 1944 by a new boiler built by Vulcan Iron Works in Vancouver.

Master spent much of her life towing for the Master Towing Company. In 1940, she was purchased by the Marpole Towing Company and towed coal barges from Vancouver Island to Vancouver. However, by 1959, Evans, Coleman, and Evans, who had taken over Marpole, decided to dispense with its "old-timers," tying them up at the mouth of the Pitt River and leaving them to the forces of nature. By 1962, *Master* had deteriorated badly and was put up for sale: "As is, where is."

According to Doug, she was seen by members of the World Ship Society of Western Canada, a branch of an organization based in England and subsequently purchased for $500. Today, *Master* is a popular and cherished historic vessel on the West Coast. In 1967, she was turned over to a society dedicated specifically to her restoration and preservation (called, appropriately, the SS Master Society).

"She's carried the Canadian flag to steam meets in the San Juan Islands, down to Seattle, Washington, and virtually every

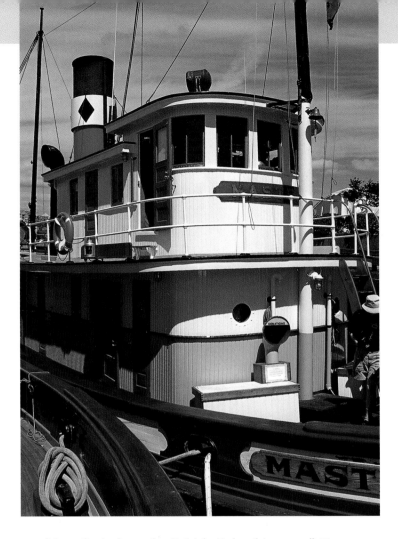

YEAR:	1922
DESIGNER:	Arthur Moscrop
BUILDER:	Arthur Moscrop, Beach Avenue Shipyard, Vancouver, British Columbia
LENGTH:	85 feet
BEAM:	20 feet
DRAFT:	12 feet
ORIGINAL POWER:	Triple expansion steam engine, built in Scotland, 1916
CURRENT POWER:	Same
CONSTRUCTION:	Fir on fir
HOME PORT:	Vancouver, British Columbia

maritime festival on the British Columbia coast," Doug says proudly. "And because now she's retired, she's registered as a steam yacht—which means that every year she has to pass the coast guard inspection."

Doug adds that it seems her crew spends more time working on her boiler than they do steaming it. He also points out that three levels of the Canadian government have contributed to saving and maintaining this historic vessel, as well as many or-

ganizations and companies in Canada and the United States. "It's all being done in the belief that the preservation of this example of our maritime history is worth the effort."

The true beauty of the *Master* is that her sole purpose is to allow lovers of wooden boats—whether casual or terminally committed—to experience steamboating as it was done nearly a century ago. Her decks and companionways are open to the public whenever she attends a wooden boat festival. Her crew, consisting of retired seamen and tugboat captains, answers questions and explains or demonstrates her amazing features. Like any tug, she is primarily an engine room and a small steering station, with minimal quarters and galley for crew. The size and depth of her engine room, the heat created by her boiler, and the ferocity of steam power are impressive. At one baritone blast of the *Master*'s steam horn, visitors grimace with amazement and admiration. Eager tugboat aficionados from Pender Harbour to Victoria await her coming every summer.

Mavourneen

Charles Royce

Watch Hill, Rhode Island

Mavourneen was built in 1930 at the Camper/Nicholson yard in England. The Nicholson family used her as a tender for its 8-meter sailing yacht. According to the boat's full-time guardian, Captain Kirk Reynolds, Camper/Nicholson built four of these 50-foot tenders between 1923 and 1930, as well as three 40-footers.

"To my knowledge, there is only one other 50-footer existing in the States," says Kirk. "It's named *Herring Gull*, and it's located somewhere in the Carolinas."

According to Kirk, these boats were referred to as "Gelyce" tenders. The name derives from the first two letters in each of the three Nicholson brothers' wives' names.

There is no record of how this beautiful boat received such a fitting name (Kirk believes *Mavourneen* means "Irish Lassie") or an accurate history after it left the Nicholson family.

"We know at some point she had been tender to some J-boats in England, but little else. Then, after a vague period of total neglect, she ended up at Peter Freebody's Boat Shop at Hurley-on-Thames. At that point, Jim Lewis of Clayton, New York, discovered her and had Freebody restore her derelict remains."

Lewis never actually saw *Mavourneen* before or during restoration. "He first laid eyes on her when she was delivered to New York aboard a freighter in 1987," says Kirk. "Prior to that, he had only seen photographs of the boat. Lewis was an amazing collector. His boats were displayed at the Antique Museum in Clayton, New York, and at numerous shows from Ottawa to Florida."

Mavourneen's current owner, Charles Royce, purchased three boats from the Lewis collection, says Kirk, and *Mavourneen* remains one of Royce's favorites. She is currently used for dinner cruises on Long Island Sound and Narragansett Bay, and is always a participant in local boat shows.

"I've been running *Mavourneen* for over three years now," notes Kirk, "and in a variety of conditions. She tends not to be very dry. Some aspect of her design causes small beads of water to rise up and drift lazily aft to the windscreen. It's bizarre, really. Plus, she is so shallow in the forefoot that in a following sea,

Mavourneen

YEAR:	1930
DESIGNER:	Camper/Nicholson, Gosport, England
BUILDER:	Camper/Nicholson, Gosport, England
LENGTH:	50 feet
BEAM:	7 feet, 6 inches
DRAFT:	2 feet, 6 inches
ORIGINAL POWER:	6-cylinder Daimler, diesel
CURRENT POWER:	MerCruiser 8.1, gasoline
CONSTRUCTION:	Double-planked mahogany over ash and oak frames, teak superstructure, Douglas-fir decks
HOME PORT:	Watch Hill, Rhode Island

there tends to be so little buoyancy that the bow sinks in and can only be released by throttling back or going to neutral."

Mavourneen was really designed for fair weather use. "In a 1- to 2-foot chop, she handles just great. At 20 knots, she can cut through a 3-foot wake and guests aboard never notice."

Kirk admits that she does roll a little in a beam sea. At 7 feet, 6 inches at the gunwale, *Mavourneen* is a mere 6 feet, 6 inches at the waterline and less than 4 feet at the transom—which has only 4 inches in the water.

Yet, chops, beam seas, and winds were never part of the concept in a boat like *Mavourneen*. She was built for the setting sun, cocktails, and elegant dining; her open forward cockpit was meant for sheer scarves and fashionable dark glasses; her galley and saloon were designed as a respite for private affairs while anchored near a grassy riverbank. Such beautiful craftsmanship belongs in the realm of romance rather than rough sea conditions.

Merrimac

GEORGE AND PATTY BEALL

Portland, Oregon

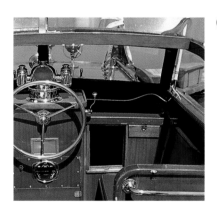

lassic yachts are sometimes called "dockside queens," a mildly derogatory term (often uttered by plastic-boat brokers) connoting a pristine varnished showpiece that seldom leaves the dock or boathouse, and rarely—if ever—sees blue water or heavy conditions. The term could easily apply to *Merrimac*, a floating classic jewel furnished with antiques and polished to perfection—yet, no notion could be more inappropriate.

George Beall of Portland, Oregon, wrote me about his classic cruiser that I might find interesting for my next book. "The boat has quite an unusual history," he explained, "and she's still very original."

I suggested a visit on one of my trips to California, but George said that it would be easier for him to stop in Anacortes, Washington, because he planned on cruising most of the summer.

"We'll go right past your neck of the woods."

In my estimation, that entailed a 100-mile run from Portland to the Columbia Bar, then a couple hundred miles in outside waters up the Washington coast to Cape Flattery, then 80 miles down the Strait of Juan de Fuca to the San Juan Archipelago, and up Rosario Strait to Anacortes Island—not impossible in a wooden boat built three quarters of a century ago, but not a Sunday outing for a dockside queen either.

I don't know what I expected when they arrived in the harbor on the west side of the island, but certainly not such a pretty, elegant, and spotless boat. *Merrimac* looked more like a contestant at a wooden boat show than the salty cruiser that had just made the trip up the coast from Portland, Oregon.

George told me that the *Merrimac* originated in the late 1930s as a Bay City Boat Inc. kit-boat called the 2200 Series Heavy-Duty Round Bottom Cruiser. According to George, the kit was ordered by Walter "Mac" McCrea, a well-known yachtsman and past commodore of the Portland Yacht Club. All of the parts and lumber were shipped from Bay City, Michigan, arriving in Portland heaped in a boxcar. As the story goes, the first boatbuilder hired to assemble the cruiser looked inside the boxcar and immediately refused the job, complaining that the project was too complicated.

Undaunted, McCrea went West to Astoria Marine Construction (AMCO) in Astoria, Oregon, and arranged an agreement with marine architect Joe Dyer: Dyer would use the kit as much as possible, but the cruiser would be built the "Astoria AMCO way." Dyer redrew the plans and used treated lumber from a local mill.

Actual construction began in early 1937. *MaryMack*, her original name, was launched on August 27, 1938, at the AMCO yard on the Lewis and Clark River in Astoria, Oregon. In 1942, the cruiser was pressed into military service—painted gray and converted to a patrol boat. According to local folklore, a 50-caliber machine gun was mounted on her foredeck and, for several years, *MaryMack* patrolled off the Oregon Coast out of Nehalem Bay.

After World War II, the cruiser was purchased by Charlie Wegman, a Portland construction company owner. He renamed the boat *Dee Dee Jo* after his two daughters and cruised her until about 1950. Under Wegman's stewardship, the gray paint was finally removed. Horace Williams, owner of the popular Tik Tok restaurant in Portland, was the cruiser's next owner, renaming her *Princess*. Williams maintained the boat until 1953.

In 1953, the cruiser returned to its place of origin and became Dyer's personal yacht, which he renamed *Merrimac*. Dyer added the boat's flybridge in 1953 and his trademark brow over the reconfigured windshield. From bow to stern, the bilges were wrapped in iron bark for protection from floating debris and ice. The original Chrysler Royal Crown engine was replaced with a Buda diesel. According to the yacht's current owner, Dyer and AMCO are today recognized as one of the highest quality West Coast boatbuilders. In fact, Dyer is currently the only marine architect featured at the Columbia River Maritime Museum. The Bay City Boat Inc. catalog, original kit drawings, and revised AMCO drawings are all still kept aboard the boat.

In her heyday, *Merrimac* was known locally as the Million Dollar Yacht, and a peek inside her interior easily explains why. Her first unique feature is a large combination head-shower in the very forward of the boat. As you step below to the forward stateroom from the pilothouse via an entry to port, there are large beveled-glass book cabinets. The forward cabin is roomy with generous storage space and bunks and seating to starboard. You then step down into the large head, which leads to a full-size shower stall still situated lower than the forward head. Headroom is excellent throughout the interior. The design makes sense when the boat is viewed from the outside: the forward raised-trunk cabin is at the same level as the aft cabin—traditional raised-deck cruisers of that period typically had flush forward decks and butterfly skylights to create headroom.

Merrimac's pilothouse is also unique. To starboard of the steering station is a large and comfortable single settee. The steering station retains the original fixtures and controls, offset only by newer navigational aids. The large settee abaft the steering station enables passengers to "ride in style" with full view while underway.

Abaft the pilothouse by starboard is the gorgeous and completely original galley, with a large comfortable dinette opposite for four or even six. Farther aft is a large double stateroom and head, with stairs up to an open cockpit.

The varnished interior of this boat, the color schemes, the lighting, and the framed photographs and memorabilia that George has added make the interior of *Merrimac* feel more like a museum. In fact, George keeps the boat in the original Portland boathouse that her first owner built, and part of it has been turned into a small nautical museum.

In 1971, Dyer sold *Merrimac* to Jim Stacy, a sawmill and tugboat company owner from Astoria. Stacy maintained and cruised the boat for twenty-three years; his logbooks show trips that circumnavigated Vancouver Island, cruised the San Juan Islands, and trekked as for north as Alaska. During his years of ownership, the boat was repowered with its present engine, a 450 Cummins V-8 diesel.

Her current owner acquired *Merrimac* in October 1994.

Merrimac

YEAR:	1938
DESIGNER:	Bay City Boat Inc. and Joe Dyer
BUILDER:	Astoria Marine Construction, Astoria, Oregon
LENGTH:	45 feet
BEAM:	11 feet, 6 inches
DRAFT:	3 feet, 6 inches
ORIGINAL POWER:	Chrysler Royal Crown, gasoline
CURRENT POWER:	V-8 450 Cummins, diesel
CONSTRUCTION:	Mahogany carvel planks over bent-oak frames, spruce decks
HOME PORT:	Portland, Oregon

Fortunately, the boat has always been exceptionally maintained and continues to be so to an even higher standard, inside and out. With attention to original design and period, George created an interior hunting-den theme featuring duck decoys, mounted shotguns, leather upholstery, hunter-green carpet, varnished mahogany, and polished chrome. Much of the interior remains original, including hand pumps in both heads, and fixtures throughout. The original solid-mahogany galley table—for years hidden under a layer of Formica—was recently restored to its original luster and embellished with a gold-leaf design.

A tribute to the concept of stewardship and high quality craftsmanship, *Merrimac* is a member of both the Antique and Classic Boat Association and the Pacific Northwest Classic Yacht Association.

Nan

STEVE HEMRY AND DIANE ANDERSON

Everett, Washington

Everyone who buys a wooden boat inherits a small legacy, whether they recognize the legacy right away or find it only after they've owned the boat a while. "We were sailboat people," says Diane Anderson. "My husband Steve Hemry and I were looking around for a fiberglass sailboat to live aboard. Steve accidentally came across an old wooden boat with a 'for sale' sign taped on the hull. It obviously needed a ton of work, but Steve thought it would be much roomier to live aboard than a sailboat. At that point, we were completely clueless about *Nan*'s history or the legacy that was being dumped in our laps. We were sailboaters. We came from a different world, right? Who's Ed Monk?"

As most wooden boat owners know, Ed Monk was a premier naval architect early in the twentieth century. He's credited with creating more than three thousand naval designs ranging from pleasure cruisers to fishing vessels to sailboats. Surviving Monk boats are some of the most beautiful, most sought after, and most functional boats afloat. Bet Oliver's book, *Ed Monk and the Tradition of Classic Boats*, chronicles his life and achievements with hundreds of photographs and testimonials from people who knew and worked with him. The back cover of the book has a famous photograph of Ed Monk next to one of *Nan*.

Nan

YEAR:	1934
DESIGNER:	Ed Monk Sr., Seattle, Washington
BUILDER:	Ed Monk Sr. and Arthur Monk, Seattle, Washington
LENGTH:	50 feet
BEAM:	14 feet, 3 inches
DRAFT:	3 feet, 5 inches
ORIGINAL POWER:	Kermath, gasoline
CURRENT POWER:	Ford Lehman, diesel
CONSTRUCTION:	Double-planked cedar and fir over oak frames
HOME PORT:	Everett, Washington

The boat's previous owner told Diane and Steve that she was once owned by Ed Monk, but it had no significance for them. "We didn't know anything about Monk, so his comment didn't impress us. We just had our hearts set on buying this old wooden boat—actually, Steve did—but the owner seemed reluctant to sell her even though she was clearly for sale. It wasn't about price, either. He just seemed very attached to *Nan*. We later discovered that another party was trying to buy the boat at the same time, and I guess their financing didn't go through; finally, after weeks and weeks, the boat became ours."

Today, *Nan* has been restored to remarkable perfection and charm. Gazing around at the interior—which remains almost exactly the same as when Monk lived aboard with his family—you feel transported back in time.

"It had been out of the water for a long time," Diane says. "so when it was put back into the water it leaked badly. When we went out for a ride with the previous owner, I thought we were going to sink. But Steve could somehow see past all that, and I guess I agreed. *Nan* is such a beautiful boat to look at because of her lines and low profile. Plus, her interior space is so well thought out as a liveaboard."

During the late 1920s and early 1930s, Ed Monk was a young shipwright and designer employed by the famous naval architect L. E. "Ted" Geary. It was the Roaring Twenties, and Geary was designing boats for famous Hollywood luminaries such as John Barrymore (see at the *Thea Foss*). During the Depression years that followed, Monk made the difficult decision to strike out on his own to design his own boats. He had a family and little money, so he built a boat that they could live aboard full-time, including space for his small office.

"Ed and his family lived aboard the *Nan* for approximately five years. She was berthed at the Seattle Yacht Club. Monk began his independent career designing boats in that small office space right over there," Diane says, pointing to the port corner of the pilothouse and saloon. "From that spot, Ed launched a thirty-six-year career that produced over 3,100 naval designs."

Wandering through this compact cruiser, you appreciate Monk's foresight and practicality. The forward cabin—typically set up as a V-berth stateroom on most bridge decks—has a spacious galley to both port and starboard, with a small but comfortable dinette forward. The galley's roominess, generous headroom, and small dinette make it an ideal living space.

The combination saloon and steering station is bright and airy, with huge windows, a comfortable sofa to starboard, and a built-in china closet and buffet aft, next to Ed's drafting table. A companionway to starboard leads aft through a narrow passageway to the current master stateroom to port, which is followed by the head and a large second stateroom aft.

"I guess the discovery came about slowly over several years," says Diane. "People kept coming by and telling us what we

had. No matter where we went with her, someone would come down to the docks who knew the boat had been Ed Monk's original liveaboard."

One day, someone gave them a notice torn out of a boating magazine: "If you own a Monk boat or have knowledge of one, please write to Bet Oliver in Canada."

"I thought it would be fun," says Diane, "so I wrote her, never dreaming that *Nan* would become one of the focal points of her book."

Diane explains that the restoration of their boat actually began in 1994, immediately after they bought her. "Initially, we

thought we could just put in some new batteries and slap on some fresh paint. But once the restoration began, there was no end to it. It took us seven years." *Nan* landed in good hands: Diane makes her living designing and decorating boat interiors and Steve is a professional surveyor.

"Steve and I work well together. I know what a ⁵⁄₁₆-inch wrench is, and he knows how to paste wallpaper. We both have had a hand in every inch of this seven-year process; however, he did all the plumbing, wiring, and engine work—with occasional assistance from me. He also made the blueprints (in his head) for the layout in the engine room. I did the interior painting and vinyl wall covering, stripped and varnished, and cleaned the bilge with some assistance from Steve. We cut and installed all the vinyl and carpet and padding. The exterior was done by both of us, including six weeks last year spent refastening the boat and painting the hull."

Diane has dozens of stories of admirers telling them about *Nan*'s history. "Once, while cruising in the South Sound, Ed Monk's only surviving daughter, Isabel, came aboard the boat with her husband, Joe. She brought us a lantern that her father had given her, which was used as the original anchor light. I've placed it above the buffet. Isabel was so pleased to see that we were taking good care of *Nan*. It was the first time she had been aboard the boat since when she was a teenager. She knew her father was smiling down on us from somewhere."

Diane and Steve now live aboard *Nan* full-time, cruising Puget Sound and the San Juan Islands and attending wooden boat festivals. In the summer of 2001, *Nan* was judged Best Power Boat at the Victoria Wooden Boat Show.

"The judges came aboard and looked around very favorably," says Diane. "Then, one of them climbed below to see our engine room. When he came up, he insisted that each of the other judges climb down in there. They all came up smiling."

Nisca

FREDERICK AND REBECCA CROSBY

Old Lyme, Connecticut

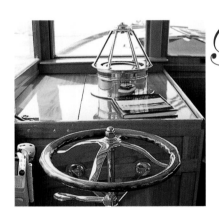

Because of her slender ducktail stern section and low profile of her trunk cabin, you don't expect the boat to be so roomy and comfortable when you step aboard the Piute Class Express Cruiser *Nisca*. You quickly discover that it has been designed to make the most of a classic cruiser just 40 feet long with a beam of only 9 feet, 6 inches.

The comfort begins in the aft cabin, accessible from both the main saloon and the aft deck companionways. This spacious sleeping compartment, with excellent headroom and portlights, has comfortable bunks on both sides, a large head to starboard between the cabin and the pilothouse, and a shower and narrow hanging closet opposite. The pilothouse is roomy and airy—with large windows all around—and the steering station to port includes replicas of the original control levers polished to perfection. Forward and below is a huge galley to either side, followed by a large saloon and eventually a forecastle cabin with an extremely attractive head.

Nisca's owners have gone to extremes to restore this beautiful boat: it doesn't seem possible that it has been around for more than three quarters of a century. Her restoration is so exquisite and her varnished joinery so splendid that it feels like you are standing inside a new boat.

Nisca

YEAR:	1924
DESIGNER:	William Hand Jr.
BUILDER:	Portland Yacht Yard, Portland, Connecticut
LENGTH:	40 feet
BEAM:	9 feet, 6 inches
DRAFT:	3 feet, 6 inches
ORIGINAL POWER:	Sterling FS, gasoline
CURRENT POWER:	Turbo Intercooled Isuzu MTC3
CONSTRUCTION:	Cedar planking over oak frames, teak house
HOME PORT:	Old Lyme, Connecticut

Topsides are just as breathtaking in appearance. Her decks, brightwork, bronze portlights and hardware, and unique outside steering station—located abaft the pilothouse—make this "bygone yacht" feel more like a floating wooden sculpture than a "boat."

North Star II

ALAN AND BARBARA ALMQUIST

Isleton, California

North Star II is an excellent example of the Stephens Brothers boats built during the 1920s in Stockton, California. Her rich teak cabins and bronze hardware and portlights, contrasted with white canvas top decks and natural teak side walkways, render this bridge-deck cruiser a wood-lover's dream. Built on contract in 1928 for Sam Heyman, of San Francisco, California, her original cost was a mere $14,000. Heyman specified that her hull be fastened with brass screws, rather than nailed—a decision that clearly added to her longevity.

Heyman, who named the boat *Alice*, sold her in 1931, after which she had a dozen different owners and various names before the Almquists bought her in 1984. They renamed her *North Star II* and began the major restoration efforts evident in the cruiser today. Her hull was refastened, most framing was replaced, and the interior of the yacht was completely refurbished. During the 1950s, the Scripps engines were replaced with twin Chrysler Crowns, which are freshwater-cooled using piping that runs along the outside of the hull, both port and starboard. In 1993, the entire transom section of the boat was replaced.

Aboard *North Star II*, her interior brightwork is meticulous yet original in every way. The double berths forward are accented by original

lighting fixtures. The steering and control station to port in the pilothouse retain the Chrysler Crown gauges, along with professionally installed electrical panels and operating controls. The traditional Stephens main cabin—the galley to port, an enclosed head to starboard, a bunk-settee abaft the head, and a bulkhead that has been opened between the galley and a small dinette—is both comfortable and roomy. The parquet flooring enhances the varnished teak interior, and leads aft to a covered cockpit area with clear-vinyl side curtains. From a distance, the obvious Stephens design—plumb bow, long forward deck, and choppy house and saloon—embodies the characteristics of a Roaring Twenties classic yacht. Her twin Chrysler Crowns, still running great after nearly half a century, produce that deep water-cooled exhaust rumble that classic enthusiasts love to hear.

Norwester

KENT KIEFER

Roche Harbor, Washington

Old logbooks of the *Norwester* record the names of regular guests, which included Hollywood celebrities, among them Bette Davis, Charlton Heston, Orson Wells, Roger Corman, Richard Wagner, Ward Bond, and Ray Milland.

Built in 1932 at the Willis J. Reid Shipyard in Winthrop, Massachusetts, just outside of Boston, *Norwester* made her way to Hollywood in 1937, settling in San Pedro, California. During World War II she was commandeered by the U.S. Navy to serve as a coastal patrol vessel. After the war, she was repowered with Detroit 671s and purchased in 1953 by a well-known—and well-connected—Hollywood film agent, Boo Roos. During the 1940s and 1950s, one of Roos's clients was film legend John Wayne. Because of his Hollywood cowboy persona, Wayne's fans imagined that his private life naturally involved horses and ranching. Yet nothing could be farther from fact: when asked by Johnny Carson if he enjoyed horseback riding in his leisure time, the Duke snarled, "The only reason I ever get on a horse is to make money!" In real life, John Wayne was actually passionately devoted to boating, and his agent Boo Roos and the *Norwester* were responsible.

Like dozens of other young clients, Wayne was frequently invited aboard Roos's boat during the 1940s. However, cruising became an instant

fascination for the Duke—so much so that by 1953, he convinced Roos to make him a partner in the boat. Wayne cruised *Norwester* for the next ten years, during which time he had the entire roof of the saloon raised a full 12 inches to accommodate his 6-foot, 4-inch height. Like most avid boaters, his passion eventually developed into long-range cruising. In 1963, he purchased a converted Canadian minesweeper from Max Wyman and named it *Wild Goose*. Wayne sold his share of *Norwester* back to Roos. The boat remained in the Roos family even after Boo's death.

When you step aboard, you can easily envision yourself living here full-time, due in part to the roominess. This solid wooden classic cruiser with a painted and varnished exterior lives outside year-round rather than in a protected boathouse like most classics. The walkaround decks, covered aft and forward to the pilothouse, are designed for strolling. The foredeck is huge, bright, and glossy, with lustrous mahogany brightwork. The pilothouse has the distinct feel of a seagoing vessel that could plow north through the most difficult conditions. The controls and instrument panel exhibit the clean, spartan, and

Norwester

YEAR:	1932
DESIGNER:	Frank Monroe
BUILDER:	Willis J. Reid Shipyard, Winthrop, Massachusetts
LENGTH:	76 feet
BEAM:	16 feet, 6 inches
DRAFT:	6 feet
ORIGINAL POWER:	Twin Winton, diesel
CURRENT POWER:	Twin Detroit 671 (circa 1945)
CONSTRUCTION:	Ash over oak frames
HOME PORT:	Roche Harbor, San Juan Island, Washington

functional design that runs through the entire vessel. It is impossible to stand behind the captain's chair without envisioning the Duke himself at the controls, with the custom wet bar he had installed abaft the steering station to port. However, the real fascination with this boat is her interior layout. Descending the short stairway starboard from the pilothouse, you enter the main saloon (with more than ample headroom), furnished and decorated exactly as it may have been when Roos and Wayne owned the boat. This 1930s-era Hollywood style, consistent throughout the boat, is more straightforward than glitzy or art deco, as one might expect in a classic yacht with a film-star-studded history. The furnishings, photographs of the Duke, occasional antique rifles, and the lighting seem appropriate to *Norwester*'s history.

The master cabin is aft and down a steep ladder. The furniture and head with built-in tub and shower are original and perfectly consistent with the boat. But the jewel of this craft is in her galley and dining saloon, located below and forward of the pilothouse. This section is entered from the main saloon via a stairway to port. The lower saloon, with built-in table and seating, is ideal for reading, writing, or watching old John Wayne videos. A huge skylight overhead makes this room bright and comfortable. The forward galley is spacious, stretching to both port and starboard. There is a forward sleeping compartment and a large, comfortable stateroom aft of the lower saloon. The hallway running along the lower portside leads to the huge engine room.

Norwester's home port today is Roche Harbor, on Washington's San Juan Island. Her current owner, music-industry executive Kent Kiefer, divides his time between Napa, California, and the San Juan Islands, living most of the summer aboard *Norwester*. He is fascinated with the boat and her Hollywood history, and plans to restore and care for her mechanically and structurally, while keeping her just as she was when the Duke owned the boat.

Olympus

John and Diane VanDerbeek

Seattle, Washington

People dream of yachts: lounging on spacious fantail aft decks, leaning against varnished teak rails and watching the sunset, sleeping in a private cabin, and listening to the waves tap the hull. This is a book for those dreamers.

Dreamers were on my mind the day Kathy and I were invited aboard the beautiful and stately fantail *Olympus*. Originally christened *Junaluska*, she was custom-designed and built by New York Yacht, Launch & Engine Company in 1929 for George Heck, who later became president of the New York Stock Exchange. Typical of many of the marvelous boats built in 1929, *Junaluska* changed owners frequently during the traumatic 1930s. She was eventually purchased for silent-film star Mary Stewart by her husband, who brought the boat to the West Coast. During World War II, she was commandeered by the armed forces, and her magnificent varnished exterior was painted gray and war guns were mounted on her decks.

After the war, the boat was obtained by the State of Washington Department of Fish and Wildlife to be used as a patrol vessel. However, according to her current owners, John and Diane VanDerbeek, the events

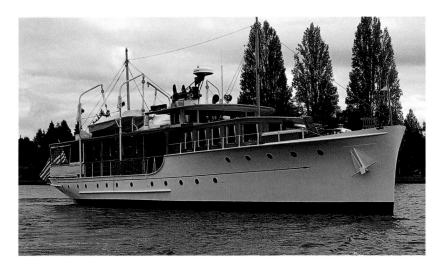

surrounding the *Olympus* at that point become rather shadowy. She became the focus of a huge political scandal involving the governor of Washington, Mon Wallgren. Wallgren was a close friend of Truman, who was frequently aboard the boat for hunting and fishing excursions.

Boarding this yacht today, it's easy to appreciate her famous past: *Olympus* is decidedly "presidential," and her guest books include the signatures of President Harry Truman, many Washington State governors, Senators Warren Magnuson and Henry Jackson (the Joint Chiefs of Staff during World War II), and, more recently, former Los Angeles mayor Richard Riordan, USA Networks Inc. CEO Barry Diller, Walt Disney Co. CEO Michael Eisner, and entertainers and Hollywood celebrities Candice Bergen, Julie Andrews, Blake Edwards, Robin Williams, Al Pacino, and Hilary Swank.

"Her guest log was recently given to us by the widow of the boat's former captain, Robert Cook," says Diane. "He had carefully kept it since 1948 until it could be returned to the yacht."

Olympus

YEAR:	1929
DESIGNER:	Unknown
BUILDER:	New York Yacht, Launch & Engine Company, Morris Heights, New York
LENGTH:	97 feet
BEAM:	19 feet
DRAFT:	10 feet
ORIGINAL POWER:	Twin Winton, diesel
CURRENT POWER:	Twin Detroit 671, diesel
CONSTRUCTION:	White-fir planks over oak frames, teak house and decks
HOME PORT:	Seattle, Washington

While viewing the Rosenfeld collection of photographs at Mystic Seaport, in Mystic, Connecticut, Diane and John discovered the boat's original launching photos; framed copies are now hanging aboard *Olympus.*

The main cabin has an elegant dining room surrounded by large windows and decorated with brass lighting and framed photographs of Truman and other dignitaries. The pilothouse is located above, followed by the galley, which is accessed by a short passageway to starboard that also leads to the main saloon. Port and aft in the saloon is a staircase to the lower decks; center aft leads to the spacious fantail deck area.

Below decks, the guest cabins and large double staterooms retain the extravagant decor of decades past, complete with framed photos of Mary Stewart and historic clothing of the 1930s. The engine room of *Olympus* is as clean as most saloons, and her massive Detroit 671 diesels gleam under the fluorescent lighting.

"John and I became interested in wooden boats shortly after our marriage in 1985," says Diane. "We searched long and hard all over the country for the right boat to purchase. Then we found *Olympus* right here in Seattle, where we lived. It was difficult to buy her because her former owner really didn't want to sell her, but with persistence and the right offer, we became her proud owners on February 6, 1995."

The VanDerbeeks have done considerable work since owning the *Olympus.* "We had to have the majority of the yacht replanked, the teak decks recaulked, and the stern and fantail area replaced—twice, because the first time the yard used the wrong woods."

The VanDerbeeks also replaced the stem with purple heart. They rewired and repowered the yacht—removing her original 1929 DC panel and replacing it with an updated AC electrical panel and a new 20-kilowatt generator to complement the existing 8-kilowatt generator. In addition, they remodeled the galley

and added new appliances, while preserving the overall classic interior and exterior appearance of the yacht.

The responsibility of such a boat is not something the Van-Derbeeks take lightly, and they understand the importance of maintaining her and documenting her history. They built a huge boathouse-workshop at the docks of Lake Union Dry Dock Company on Seattle's Lake Union. *Olympus* spends the winters there, protected from the weather; summers are spent cruising Southeast Alaska and British Columbia.

O'Vation

ED AND BARB O'SULLIVAN

Seattle, Washington

The exotic woods and futuristic hull design were the first things that caught my eye when I saw *O'Vation* at a Fourth of July wooden boat show on Seattle's Lake Union.

A month later, I finally connected with the owners, Barb and Ed O'Sullivan, who were cruising north for the summer. When I explained my book project, Ed agreed to meet me at Friday Harbor late in July or early August; he was somewhere in the Gulf Islands at the time.

"What's that thing made out of?" I asked.

"Mostly rosewood," Ed replied over the cell phone. "The hull is Indonesian red nara rosewood, vacuum-bagged with Titan Epoxy to ¾-inch Knytex glass. Her stern is Honduras mahogany, and the top and side decks are Malaysian teak with rosewood accents. The interior is African ebony, rosewood, and teak."

"When was it built?"

"1986."

O'Vation may have been built in 1986, but she is aesthetically a child of the futuristic art-deco period between the world wars—a period of modernism that favored speed, chrome, black-mirror finishes, and unrestrained opulence. When we linked up at Friday Harbor, our amazement

with the boat's exterior in no way prepared us for the wooden extravagance below decks.

"She's the brainchild of Ted and DeeDee Teren," her owners told us as they invited us aboard. "They wanted to build a distinctive, fast, sexy boat. Yet, they wanted something that resembled a Garwood or an old Chris."

Ed explained that the Terens weren't afraid of fiberglass or technology or innovation—nor were they hampered by design and construction costs. They researched, consulted, and experimented, and found materials, naval architects, craftsmen, and boatyards all over the globe. The eventual result was something they called the Braginton 42.

O'Vation

YEAR:	1986
DESIGNER:	Luiz Avilliz, São Paulo, Brazil
BUILDER:	Ted Teren and Trans World Boatbuilding, Pieshy, Taiwan
LENGTH:	41 feet, 8 inches
BEAM:	11 feet, 4 inches
DRAFT:	3 feet, 4 inches
CURRENT POWER:	Twin Caterpillar 3208-TA, diesel
CONSTRUCTION:	Indonesian red nara (rosewood) hull, Honduras mahogany stern, Malaysian teak decks with rosewood accents, African ebony, rosewood, and teak interior
HOME PORT:	Seattle, Washington

"It was a prototype of what they envisioned to be a run of twenty such boats," says Ed. "This is hull #1." Due to a bizarre swindle, the Terens' production plans eventually collapsed.

Powered by 375-horsepower twin Caterpillar 3208-TA diesels, *O'Vation* has a top speed of 40 mph and cruises comfortably at 35. She planes easily at 15 mph and has a cruising range of 400 miles.

The interior of this boat is designed around the galley, as if preparing, serving, and enjoying fine meals are the reason for being below decks. You are astounded at the roominess of the main cabin—until you realize that her interior is all one cabin (except for the enclosed head). Aft, beneath the companionway ladder, is a comfortable TV parlor-lounge with sumptuous leather couches that also function as berths. The galley, stretching out to port, is a fantasy come true for every modern cook. A large formal table surrounded by circular leather seating fills the center of the main cabin, and the spacious V-berth forward has curtains for privacy.

The engine room, situated beneath the outside steering station, is as pristine and extravagant as everything else on the boat. Step inside and pat her fat-Cat diesels on the heat exchangers for assurance that the builder had the good sense to install them in a boat clearly designed for speed.

Ed says they had no intention of ever buying such a boat —they just happened to be walking on the docks of a Seattle marina and stumbled upon her. "We couldn't resist," Barb adds. "Once I went below, it was just a matter of making the arrangements."

Before leaving I stand inside gawking at the rosewood interior, the ebony trim, the abalone inlays; the degree of craftsmanship and the fine woodworking are mind-boggling.

"I have access to the plans and molds," Ed tells me. "Who knows, some day I may build another one."

Pam

BOB AND ELIZABETH TIEDEMANN

Newport, Rhode Island

Although we live in a relatively affluent society, in some ways it cannot compare with the extravagance of the 1920s. The classic commuter yacht *Pam* was built for Harrington Walker, grandson of Hiram Walker, who owned H. W. Distilleries. Harrington used *Pam* to commute to work across Lake St. Clair between Grosse Pointe, Michigan, and the shores of Ontario, Canada.

According to her current owners, Bob and Elizabeth Tiedemann, *Pam* is one of two surviving boats built by the Great Lakes Boat Building Company of Milwaukee, Wisconsin. When she was built in 1921, *Pam* was considered an engineering marvel. With her twin Sterling six-cylinder engines, narrow beam width, and 62-foot hard-chine planing hull design, she was capable of making 30 knots—an impressive speed for a boat that size even today.

Pam's current owners are not casual boaters. The couple own and operate Seascope Yacht Charters, a company that restores classic wooden yachts and offers them for charter. Bob began researching and restoring classics in 1975 when he acquired *Gleam*, a 67-foot 1937 12-meter America's Cup Class sloop. Since then, their collection has expanded to include the sailing yachts *Northern Light* (70 ft.), built in 1938; *Mariner* (54 ft.), built in 1950; and *Pam*, which Bob discovered in Florida, half sunk

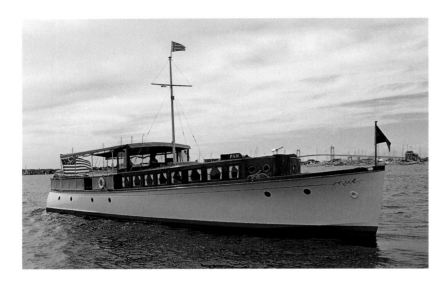

Pam

YEAR:	1921
DESIGNER:	Walter Beauvais
BUILDER:	Great Lakes Boat Building Company, Milwaukee, Wisconsin
LENGTH:	62 feet
BEAM:	12 feet
DRAFT:	4 feet
ORIGINAL POWER:	6-cylinder twin Sterling
CURRENT POWER:	Twin V-8 Marine Power
CONSTRUCTION:	Double-planked mahogany hull, inner planks diagonal on oak frames, outer planks carvel matched mahogany, pine decks, mahogany house
HOME PORT:	Newport, Rhode Island

with both engines seized, the foredeck caved in, and much of the house and interior suffering from rot.

Today, the elegance and charm of this unique boat disguise the state of neglect in which she was found. The exterior brightwork, chromed hardware and deck fittings, and sheer of her hull rival any wooden classic afloat. *Pam*'s aft deck, with a fully extendable canvas top and transparent roll-down side curtains, is the epitome of summer cruising comfort. The wicker furniture and leather-covered cushions can accommodate literally dozens of guests. *Pam* is unique in that, unlike most classic yachts designed to sleep as many people as possible, her interior space is more conducive to social events. The steering station, located amidships to port, is open. A center companionway leads below with a large

pantry to port, opposite the galley—still entirely original. A narrow passageway, with the head to port, leads to an immense saloon area for dining, socializing, or sleeping. A hatch leads to the foredeck with a skylight overhead, and a crew cabin is located forward.

The engine room is abaft the steering station and accessible via a lift-up compartment cover that also serves as seating in the aft deck area. The only other sleeping accommodation is the modestly sized two-bunk cabin, accessed by lifting a large hatch in the flush deck.

There is more to *Pam*'s charm than her spacious decks, comfortable saloon, and gleaming elegance. Her grace and comfort underway, the sleekness of her narrow hull, and the simplicity of her design make this classic exceptional at any gathering of restored wooden boats. The Tiedemanns are committed to maintaining their fleet of pristine wooden yachts—which surpasses every wooden boat aficionado's wildest dreams—and *Pam* is clearly the pride of their achievements.

Parry

BOB AND KATHY JORDAN

Vancouver, British Columbia

The *Parry* and the *Union Jack* (see page 165) are two stately old tugs that slowly meander through the Inside Passage each summer, calling at ports in Bella Bella, Prince Rupert, and Langara on the extreme tip of the Queen Charlottes. They poke along at 8 knots, operating on slow-turn diesel engines, ghosting into remote inlets to drop anchor for the night and provide a base camp for sportfishers or whalewatchers. Built in 1941, the *Parry* and the *Union Jack* were designed as working tugboats for the waters of the Pacific Northwest, and both continue today in much the same tradition. Other than lighter cargoes and more attractive and comfortable accommodations, they are the same boats plying the same waters of the rugged British Columbia coast, as slowly and surely as they did more than sixty years ago.

In the early 1900s, tugboats were originally powered by immense, cumbersome steam engines. By the 1920s, the slow-turn diesel combustion engine had replaced steam, but the new engines were still massive and similar to steam engines: rocker arms and valves had to be constantly oiled, and cams and starting gears were operated manually. Slow-turn diesels, like the Vivian diesel still powering the *Parry* and the Goliath 400-horsepower Union still powering the *Union Jack*, came without any gearbox; they are direct-drive from the crankshaft to the prop, which means no neutral or reverse.

Parry

YEAR:	1941
DESIGNER:	Unknown
BUILDER:	Armstrong Brothers, Victoria, British Columbia
LENGTH:	84 feet
BEAM:	21 feet
DRAFT:	8 feet
ORIGINAL POWER:	Vivian, diesel
CURRENT POWER:	Same
CONSTRUCTION:	Fir planks and fir decks
HOME PORT:	Vancouver, British Columbia

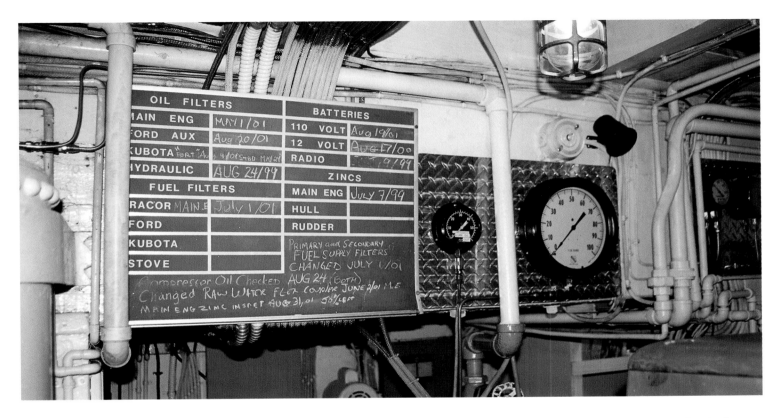

OIL FILTERS		BATTERIES	
MAIN ENG	MAY 1/01	110 VOLT	Aug 19/01
FORD AUX	Aug 20/01	12 VOLT	Aug 17/00
KUBOTA	FORT Aug 4/01 STBD MAY 21	RADIO	9/99
HYDRAULIC	AUG 24/99	ZINCS	
FUEL FILTERS		MAIN ENG	July 7/99
RACOR MAIN E	July 1/01	HULL	
FORD		RUDDER	
KUBOTA		PRIMARY and SECONDARY FUEL SUPPLY FILTERS CHANGED JULY 1/01	
STOVE			

Compressor Oil Checked AUG 24 (both)
Changed Raw Water Fler Couplere June 2/01 M.E
MAIN ENG ZINC INSPET AUG 31, 01 50% LEFT

"It's a matter of practice," says Michael Boskovich, skipper of the *Parry*. "That and always planning your moves well ahead of time."

"The prop can only be reversed when the engine is stopped and shut off," says Michael, "and then restarted in the opposite direction. This is accomplished by shifting the camshaft, which has two different sets of lobes: one set for ahead and an identical set for reverse. Once the engine is dead-stopped, the cam is moved onto the new lobes. Then air is injected into the appropriate cylinder to push the piston down in the opposite direc-

tion; when fuel is applied, the engine restarts, running in the opposite direction."

According to Michael, these engines typically weigh approximately 20 tons or more and operate at about 340 rpm, cruising at 8 or 8½ knots.

"They run forever," Michael adds. "As long as they're oiled and properly maintained, there's virtually no limit to their life span."

Having already purchased and restored the *Union Jack*, by the late 1980s Bob and Kathy Jordan had their eyes on a second boat.

"We'd known of the *Parry* since the 1970s," Kathy says. "Her condition was very poor. When her owner passed away, the boat was offered to us, but at the time we said no."

But by the mid-1980s, the Jordans felt they could expand their sportfishing charters with an additional boat. "The *Parry* was still available," says Bob. "But she would take an unbelievable amount of work. All of her decking was soft, all of the deck beams from the house to the stern had to be replaced. The tops of her tanks were rusted through. She eventually needed fourteen planks on the hull."

The condition of the engine room was terrible, a murky quagmire of oil and sludge.

"The *Parry* was built for the Canadian navy reserve in 1941," says Bob. "She was used as a towing and patrol boat during World War II and then was sold to the Canadian Hydrographic Service in 1948."

Both vessels had virtually no downtime throughout their entire lives, operating year-round, decade after decade.

The *Parry*, like the *Union Jack*, is a blend of hominess, antiquity, and functionality. Her engine room, with its massive Vivian diesel, is a testimony to the Jordans' resolve to restore and preserve historic wooden vessels while continuing to use them as workboats. The *Parry*'s configuration, like that of the *Union Jack*, accommodates travelers below in traditional double-bunk compartments, while the main deck has a large social cabin and a spacious galley. The pilothouse up top retains all of the original controls, fixtures, and navigation equipment, as well as the marvelous oak chart table.

The Jordans readily admit that they could have chosen an easier path in life. Modern vessels to live aboard and from which to make their living would be less expensive and less work. The maintenance of the tugs requires considerable planning and knowledge.

Bob points out that old wooden tugs have advantages that

other boats don't, however. "They're lower to the water," he says. "They have massive tankage for long-term operation. Their main decks have far more room than traditional fishing boats. Plus, I wouldn't get on an aluminum or steel boat. I grew up with wooden boats, net lofts, manila ropes, and big diesel engines. And I was lucky enough to marry a woman who feels the same way about wooden boats. And that's been the real key to it all."

Pat Pending

MEL AND GIG OWENS

Belvedere, California

In June 1997, the beautiful 50-foot classic yacht *Pat Pending* was found half-submerged at her berth and about to settle to the bottom of San Francisco Bay. A naturally occurring calamity below the waterline known as "keel-hogging" was ending her life—or so it seemed. Emergency crews pumped out the water and contained the oil that swirled through the interior as the engine filled with salt water. She was immediately towed to Sausalito and hauled at the Richardson Bay Boatworks. The prognosis was not good.

Originally owned by movie producer Lloyd Bacon (in 1927, he made the first "talkie": *The Jazz Singer*, starring Al Jolson), *Pat Pending* was constructed in Seattle, Washington, by the Lake Union Dry Dock Company in 1929. Christening her *Lightnin* at the time of her launch, Bacon affectionately nicknamed his yacht "Mammy" after Jolson's famous film rendition of the song. Over the years, Jolson was a regular crew member on the boat, and "Mammy" would eventually host Hollywood luminaries, including Bing Crosby and Humphrey Bogart.

Built as a 45-footer, "Mammy" saw her first major refit in 1931, when she was lengthened an additional 5 feet. According to lore, when first owner Lloyd Bacon wasn't producing movies, he was an avid predicted-log racer.

After increasing his boat's length, he entered a predicted-log race between Long Beach and San Francisco, losing the navigation skills race to a technicality. Bacon reportedly became so disgusted that he walked away from the dock in San Francisco and never saw his boat again. It was sold that year to San Franciscan Ellis Arkrush, then a few years later to a lawyer, Eugene Bennett. But by 1940, "Mammy" found what appears to be her permanent home: she was purchased by A. Donham Owen, a San Francisco patent attorney who renamed her *Pat Pending*. She has remained in the Owen family ever since.

Today, this marvelous cruiser is more pristine, more attractive, and dependably more functional than at any time in her long and active life.

"The near-sinking in 1997 required considerable discussion on the part of the family," says her current owner, Mel Owen, Don's son (also a San Francisco attorney). As a young boy, he remembers being aboard the boat for an outing on San Francisco Bay on December 7, 1941.

"We heard on the radio that the Japanese had bombed Pearl Harbor. We returned to our berth at the Oakland Yacht Club, and went on patrol that night with the coast guard auxiliary. The next morning, Dad got a call from the navy, requiring delivery of *Pat Pending* to Treasure Island by twelve noon the next day."

Like many sizable pleasure boats throughout the area, *Pat Pending* spent the next two and a half years patrolling the submarine nets strung inside the Golden Gate. She was painted gray and fitted with deck artillery and depth charges.

After the war, the boats conscripted by the government were auctioned off to the highest bidder. This concerned Don Owen, as he felt it was only fair to offer the conscripted boats to their original owners first. Congress agreed, passing Public Law 305 in 1944, which required the navy to offer the now-surplus and badly battered boats to their prewar owners first. *Pat Pend-*

ing was the first boat returned under the new law, and she was restored over the next nine months at a cost of $24,000.

"My father believed in this boat very strongly," says Mel. "He wanted his children to grow up enjoying her and learning the ways of the sea and family boating."

The same logic prevailed in 1997, Mel explains with a touch of humor. He recalls calling together his sons, Greg and Lawson, for a meeting at the Tadich Grill in San Francisco. "I told the boys that when I'm gone, they could either have an inheritance check or the boat."

There was never any question: the decision was made not only to repair the boat, but also to restore her completely.

"We started with the keel and went from there," says Mel. "We felt that Ross Sommers of Richardson Bay Boatworks had both the knowledge and the expert team of woodworkers re-

Pat Pending

YEAR:	1929
DESIGNER:	L. E. "Ted" Geary
BUILDER:	Lake Union Dry Dock Company, Seattle, Washington
LENGTH:	50 feet
BEAM:	11 feet, 7 inches
DRAFT:	4 feet, 6 inches
ORIGINAL POWER:	Hall Scott Invader
CURRENT POWER:	Same
CONSTRUCTION:	Carvel-planked 1¼-inch fir (new) over 1½-inch bent-oak frames, teak superstructure
HOME PORT:	Belvedere, California

quired to do the job, so we committed to completely rebuilding the boat. We had no choice, really. She had been a family tradition for over fifty-seven years."

Rebuilding *Pat Pending* ultimately entailed replacing every frame and every plank, rebuilding the Hal Scott engine, and replacing all decks and supporting deck beams. Eventually,

Carl Schumacher, a noted marine architect, was contracted to re-design the forward and aft cabins. Such an undertaking naturally included replacing all wiring, plumbing, and tanks, as well as applying copious paint and varnish.

Today, it's difficult to imagine this boat with guns mounted on her decks, and it's impossible to detect that she had ever threatened to sink. The teak joinery work in her forward cabins, the brass lighting fixtures (re-created from antiques), the teak and holly cabin soles, the well-thought-out placement of modern navigation instruments and upgraded controls in the pilothouse—all are clearly the work of top-level marine craftspeople. The stanchions, handrails, toerails, and rubrails; the white decks and brightwork topside; the hardware and windlass are—in a word—exquisite.

Located aft of the pilothouse via a centerline companionway, the galley to port is spacious. The aft cabin itself is huge, designed for social comfort rather than multiple sleeping berths. The covered cockpit is comfortable with cushioned seating all around and a center drop-leaf table. Unique to this boat is a companionway from the bridge to the upper deck above the saloon, where there is additional outdoor seating, both port and starboard, as well as a flybridge steering station.

After corresponding with Mel and Gig Owen, I met them at a small marina on the San Joaquin Delta where they berth their boat in the summer. It was hot and very windy, which Mel explained was quite normal for August in that area. Regardless of the high winds, they insisted on taking the boat out and showing us the area.

"She feels new but handles exactly the same," said Mel, while at the controls. "I was insistent that her restoration accomplish that in every way."

A product of the Lake Union Dry Dock Company, the Seattle yard that coined the name "Dreamboat," *Pat Pending* has surpassed that name even in her rebirth. She's been fulfilling dreams and desires for nearly three quarters of a century and now—

thanks to the commitment, investment, and resolve of the Owen family—she'll continue doing the same for possibly another century at least. Mel and Gig Owen are keeping the legacy perfectly intact.

Pursuit Star

MARTY BOSWORTH

Seattle, Washington

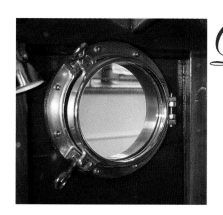

Dear Susan,

Your phone call was such a pleasant surprise. I have found an early photo (enclosed) and browsed those old logs that we have to jog my memory. It is amazing how one can forget so many of the most important moments of one's life.

During the 1940s, John G. Holstrom was the general manager of the Kenworth Trucking Company in Seattle. An avid family boater and predicted-log racer, Holstrom commissioned a Canadian shipyard in Victoria, British Columbia, to build a family cruiser—minus engine and electrical wiring. Holstrom then had the boat towed to Seattle, where he installed a Buda truck engine—taken from one of the Kenworth trucks—and completed the wiring himself. With his wife and three daughters, he cruised between Seattle and British Columbia every summer, often going as far north as Alert Bay.

"I found *Pursuit Star* by accident," says current owner, Marty Bosworth. "It was a bank repossession offer, tied up in the marina where I stay during the summer. It was love at first sight."

Bosworth, who works in Hollywood most of the year, spends his summers living aboard *Pursuit Star* and cruising the San Juan and Gulf Islands for several months at a time.

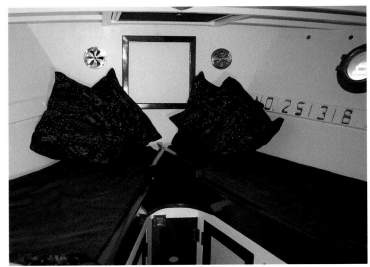

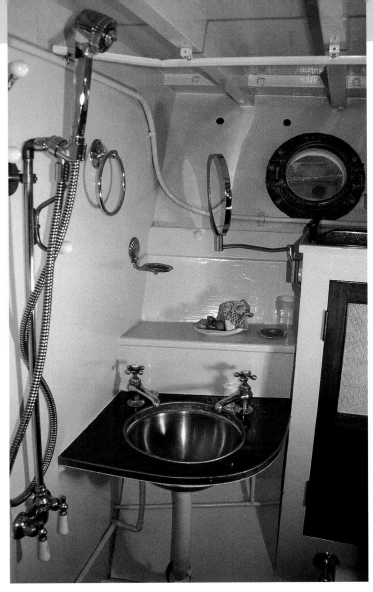

"She was originally named *Pursuit*," says Marty, "but Alex Seigo, one of her owners, changed the name to *Pursuit Star* in the 1970s."

According to Marty, Seigo moved the boat to Canada in

1976, where it remained until the late 1990s, when it was returned to the Seattle area.

"Seigo sold the boat to a couple named Anderson in 1992," says Marty. "They truly loved that boat and when I contacted them asking for some information about the boat's history, they sent me a copy of a letter they received from the original owner's daughter, Anne Hamilton. Anne still had her father's logbooks and her letter recounts the details of the boat's maiden voyage with the Buda truck engine, plus several accounts of their trips north each summer."

Marty says that the boat's successive owners believed *Pursuit Star* was designed by Ed Monk Sr. The interior is traditional, with a large saloon-galley leading to an open cockpit aft and the dinghy mounted topside. The pilothouse is spacious and bright with huge Monk-style windows raked forward. The forward cabin contains a raised V-berth with excellent storage below and an enclosed head to starboard. The flybridge was added in 1973 by A. L. Washburn, who owned the boat for only three years before selling it to Seigo—who then moved it to Canada. The joinery work throughout this boat is exquisite. The interior brightwork and white paint create the right combination of cheerfulness and antiquity, and her large Monk-style saloon-galley makes her ideal for living aboard or extended cruising.

"She's a tough little boat," says Marty. "She's proven that several times for me."

Since owning the boat, Marty has had the Detroit diesel completely rebuilt and has personally refastened and recaulked the hull.

"Her tender is cold-molded mahogany," Marty says, "and it's rather historic, I guess. It came off of John Wayne's *Wild Goose*. A previous owner, Susan Anderson, bought the dinghy as a gift for her husband Neil. They were kind enough to allow the dinghy to stay with the *Pursuit Star* when they sold her."

The value of anything is always more than the sum of its parts. It entails a myriad of intangibles, not the least of which are the memories. The letter that Susan Anderson received from the original owner's daughter describes how, in the late 1940s, they traveled to areas that few boaters reach even today—long before refrigeration, electric water pumps, or any type of navigational aids other than a compass.

The Pursuit *was used throughout the year. In the summer, we would head north, with the International Cruise Race giving us a real boost in distance. Little time was wasted getting up into the Yuculta Rapids–Stuart Island area. We explored all of the arms and inlets up there, except Knight Inlet. We even cruised up the Homathko River—the one on the left—at the head of Butte Inlet. Alert Bay was probably* Pursuit's *northern limit while we had her. It was a mighty fine life. Hope this gives you a little taste of "the olden days."—Anne Hamilton (Holstrom)*

Pursuit Star

YEAR:	1946
DESIGNER:	Ed Monk Sr. (undocumented)
BUILDER:	Falconer Marine Industries, Victoria, British Columbia
LENGTH:	38 feet
BEAM:	10 feet, 8 inches
DRAFT:	3 feet, 5 inches
ORIGINAL POWER:	Buda, gasoline
CURRENT POWER:	453 Detroit, diesel
CONSTRUCTION:	Red cedar, carvel planked over oak frames, teak decks, mahogany house
HOME PORT:	Seattle, Washington

Shahrazad

Richard M. Accola

Chester, Connecticut

The first purchase of a wooden boat is frequently the result of love at first sight. Potential enthusiasts buy *Wooden Boat Magazine,* perhaps they attend a wooden boat festival. One day they see the boat they cannot live without, and sanity is cast to the wind. Ric Accola, on the other hand, decided exactly what he wanted in a wooden boat and then began searching for a craft that fit that specific type.

"A good friend of mine owns a 1929 Elco Flattop," says Ric, "and after cruising with him several times in the summer of 1993, I decided I was crazy enough to get a wooden boat for myself."

Ric began scouting the fleet of classics attending the 1993 Antique and Classic Boat Rendezvous in Mystic, Connecticut, and eventually decided he wanted a boat like the Elco Cruisette *Skipperess* (see page 141). "The size was right, the lines were beautiful, and I loved the open cockpit in her bow."

A local wooden boat broker informed Ric that several Elco Cruisettes were on the market. "I looked at a 1926 'hunting-cabin' cruisette, as well as some later models, but finally found exactly what I was looking for—*Lucie.*"

The boat was being repaired after severe damage from a 1992 hurricane: she had been sitting in a yard on blocks when a wave knocked her off,

creating a large hole in the hull. The rudder had been torn from the transom, shattering the bronze skeg and leaving the boat partially submerged for more than two weeks. Nonetheless, *Lucie* was exactly the type of boat Ric was searching for, and he renamed her *Shahrazad* when he bought her in May 1994.

To see this boat at a classic rendezvous today, you would never guess it had suffered hurricane damage and sunk—she appears to have been stored under cover and taken out only for Sunday cruising. The interior is pristine and original, the brightwork is sparkling, the hardware gleams, and all appointments are original. Unique to the Elco design, the bow section contains a cockpit (similar to a rumble seat for two) that is accessible from the forward cabin by means of a lift-out hatch-seat. According to Ric, only the forty-five 1930 models had the front cockpit. The forward cabin is a sleeping-seating compartment with an open galley to port and an enclosed head opposite. Her pilothouse, with the original Elco-style flat-wheel steering station to port, leads to an aft saloon with large glass windows and a two-place dinette opposite the starboard settee-berth. This cabin leads to a covered aft deck. *Shahrazad*'s oriental rugs and tasteful furnishings complement her name, and the restoration is as stunning outside as it is throughout the interior. She still retains the traditional Elco production-boat simplicity that is part of its hallmark.

Ric notes that repairs from the hurricane took almost two years. "The shipwrights at Chrisholm Marina in Chester, Connecticut, repaired the keel and put the rudder and skeg assembly back together. They also repaired a hole in the transom. The electrical system was completely replaced. The galley area and stove had been under water, so the rotten counter had to be rebuilt and the rusted-out Shipmate stove had to be replaced. A new functional head was installed and the dead Chrysler Crown gasoline engine was replaced by an Isuzu diesel."

Ric adds that he recanvassed the roof and stripped the white paint off the cabin to revive the boat's mahogany brightwork. By August 1995, just three years after the hurricane nearly destroyed her, *Shahrazad* joined a fleet of classics on a six-week cruise to Canada through the Erie and Rideau Canal systems. And, in 1999, she was judged Best Elco Cruisette at the Mystic Antique and Classic Boat Rendezvous.

Shahrazad

YEAR:	1932
DESIGNER:	Glenville Tremaine, The Elco Works, Electric Boat Company, Bayonne, New Jersey
BUILDER:	The Elco Works, Electric Boat Company, Bayonne, New Jersey
LENGTH:	35 feet
BEAM:	10 feet, 3 inches
DRAFT:	2 feet, 9 inches
ORIGINAL POWER:	Elco-Buda Marine, gasoline
CURRENT POWER:	Isuzu Marine 6500-HE, diesel
CONSTRUCTION:	White-cedar planks, white-oak frames, Philippine mahogany decks and cabins
HOME PORT:	Chester, Connecticut

Skipperess

ROBERT AND ANNA SEYFRIED

Howard Beach (Jamaica Bay), New York

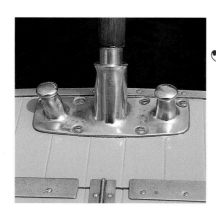

To step aboard *Skipperess* is to gain a deeper appreciation of what it means to "pay close attention to detail." There is not a bronze or brass item aboard the boat that has not been polished to a high luster. There is not an inch of mahogany that is not varnished to perfection. The brightwork and bronze hardware of her exterior gleam. It's amazing to learn that *Skipperess* has spent her entire life outside.

"Her second owner built a little frame that goes over the boat so she can be covered with canvas," says current owner, Bob Seyfried. "That was back in the 1930s. I'm still using the same frame."

Launched in 1931, *Skipperess* was built for Colgate Hoyt, a wealthy New York investment banker. Hoyt commissioned Elco Boat Works to create a model that would include a separate steering station in the open forward cockpit so that his chauffeur could "drive him around."

According to Bob and Anna Seyfried, who have owned the boat since 1966, Hoyt sold the boat in 1936 to Ambrose Day, who changed her name to *Skipperess*, which she has retained ever since.

"We had the pleasure of meeting Ambrose Day in 1981," says Bob. "*Skipperess* had won Best Motorboat at a show in Mystic Seaport, Con-

Skipperess

YEAR:	1931
DESIGNER:	The Elco Works, Electric Boat Company, Bayonne, New Jersey
BUILDER:	The Elco Works, Electric Boat Company, Bayonne, New Jersey
LENGTH:	35 feet
BEAM:	10 feet, 3 inches
DRAFT:	2 feet, 9 inches
ORIGINAL POWER:	6-cylinder Buda, gasoline
CURRENT POWER:	Chrysler Crown BM 47 "L Head"
CONSTRUCTION:	White-cedar planks over steam-bent white-oak frames, Honduras mahogany cabin and decks
HOME PORT:	Howard Beach (Jamaica Bay), New York

necticut, the year before. Ambrose saw an article about our boat in a magazine, and he called and introduced himself. He came to see the boat the next year at Mystic and told us quite a lot about her history."

Bob relates that during World War II, Ambrose Day used the *Skipperess* as a patrol boat, looking for German submarines between Block Island and Montauk Point in Rhode Island. *Skipperess* was one of the rare boats that patrolled under a private owner, rather than being commandeered into the coast guard and painted gray.

Her third owner, Ray Crosby, bought *Skipperess* in 1955. Crosby was an artist who spent his summers aboard the boat sketching in charcoal. During the winter, he would make oil paintings of the scenes and then sell them through Abercrombie and Fitch in Manhattan.

"Anna and I bought the boat in 1966," says Bob. "We are her fourth owners."

Many times over the years, they have cruised from Cape May, New Jersey, all the way to Toronto, Canada. "Lake Champlain was one of our favorite cruising areas when the kids were younger," says Bob. "People are amazed that we are still cruising after all these years. We still use the boat for fishing."

The foredeck, with her traditional anchor, polished bronze post, and bronze hawse, is classically nautical. Bob believes that the steering station in the forward cockpit is the only version in existence; it was not an Elco option, but rather a special request of the original owner when he ordered the boat. The cockpit seat, which can snugly fit three, opens in the center for access to the trunk cabin.

The forward cabin is a combination sleeping compartment, saloon, and galley, with the bunks providing seating. The galley is aft to port, with the head opposite. The pilothouse has full visibility in all directions, with a steering station to port and a single seat

for the "driver." Typical of the Elco design is the flat steering wheel and an opening port window.

The main saloon has a small dinette to port, seating to starboard, and a full-height door that opens to the aft cockpit area. The velour upholstery, curtains, fancy knotting, and lighting fixtures take visitors back in time. No matter where you sit in this little boat, you can't help focusing on the extensive detailing. Every bronze item, from cabinet hinges to air vents, is burnished bright.

"*Skipperess* is still an operational facility of the U.S. Coast Guard Auxiliary," says Bob. "She has been used to save many boats and boaters over the years. If we related all of the interesting stories, it would require an entire book." These stories would include such incidents as rescuing boaters in the Atlantic Ocean and nearly pitchpoling in Lake Ontario.

"Meeting her second owner back in 1981 had to be the highlight," says Bob. "He gave us the full history of the boat. We even have the original Elco plans, which include blueprints for every stick in the boat. Every piece of wood is numbered. When we needed to replace the 60-gallon water tank, the Elco instructions showed us exactly which pieces of wood to remove."

Bob fondly remembers that when Ambrose Day, the second owner, came aboard in 1981, he brought a sweatshirt that his wife gave him in 1937 with "Skipperess" embroidered on the front. "He was eighty years old at the time," Bob says, "and he wanted us to keep the sweatshirt on the boat. We still have it."

Spindrift II

JAYNE RABACHE AND DON SCHWARZ

Atlantic Highlands, New Jersey

Boats have their own lore, stories that follow them over the decades: amazing occurrences, dignitaries aboard, occasional brushes with disaster. During the hurricane that struck the Northeast in 1938, *Spindrift II* was snatched from her moorage on Long Island and deposited on the Westhampton Country Club golf course. In 1950, she hit a submerged jetty at the entrance to Nantucket Harbor and sank (the captain quickly deployed the dinghy and rowed the owners to safety). In 1961, while swinging at anchor at Moriches Bay on Long Island, she was hit by a speeding runabout, lost 3 feet off her bow section, and sank again.

"We are very fortunate to have a wonderful album of the boat's complete history." Her owners, Jayne Rabache and Don Schwarz, know that this record is truly a treasure. "It includes photographs, news articles of the dramatic events in the boat's life, a title abstract showing the names and dates of transfer between all ten of her previous owners, and even a collection of correspondences to and from five of them," says Jayne.

Spindrift II was built in 1929–30 by the Elco Works of the Electric Boat Company in Bayonne, New Jersey. The boat was a special-order contract for Judge Harold Medina, who at the time was a practicing New York

lawyer and professor at Columbia Law School. Medina later became a U.S. district court judge and, in 1959, authored *Anatomy of Freedom*, which recounts his distinguished career.

Judge Medina originally purchased a stock 42-foot Elco cruiser that he commissioned *Spindrift I*. However, after just a few years, he wanted a larger boat built to his specifications. At the time, Elco was adamant that it would only build boats from its stock plans, and the next model in size was 50 feet. Nevertheless, Medina was equally adamant and ultimately successful; *Spindrift II* is the only known 46-foot Elco cruiser in existence.

In today's world of sleek plastic megayachts, *Spindrift II* is an oddity. The narrow beam of 11 feet, 6 inches, the extended covering over the trunk cabin and aft deck space, the garish Cleopatra lounge mounted on top of the aft cabin next to the lapstrake dinghy—all are reminiscent of a bygone era.

"We purchased this boat sight unseen," admits Jayne. She explains that they had owned and raced a 41-foot sailing cruiser before they began their search for a classic.

"We wanted a boat that would allow us to ply the local rivers in a gracious and comfortable manner, and to cruise to ports that were otherwise impossible with the 8-foot keel of the sailboat. We learned of *Spindrift II* from other classic boat owners before she was even for sale."

When the boat came on the market at a boatyard in Jacksonville, Florida, Jayne and Don wasted no time. "We bought the boat largely on her reputation, some pictures, an in-the-water survey, and some long phone conversations with the Huckins Boatyard."

They flew to Florida and brought the boat to New Jersey up the Intracoastal Waterway—a trip *Spindrift II* had made many times before.

Spindrift II	
YEAR:	1929
DESIGNER:	The Elco Works, Electric Boat Company, Bayonne, New Jersey
BUILDER:	The Elco Works, Electric Boat Company, Bayonne, New Jersey
LENGTH:	46 feet
BEAM:	11 feet, 6 inches
DRAFT:	3 feet, 6 inches
ORIGINAL POWER:	6-cylinder twin Elco, gasoline
CURRENT POWER:	Twin 354 Perkins, diesel
CONSTRUCTION:	Cedar planks over steam-bent oak frames
HOME PORT:	Atlantic Highlands, New Jersey

"Those were truly days of delight," Jayne recalls of the journey north. "Two weeks spent prone upon the Cleopatra lounge. Even the shrimpboaters, notorious for their disdain of pleasure craft, would raise their booms, known as *arms*, to permit us safe passage, and several tossed off respectful salutes."

Spindrift II easily accommodates four people. The master stateroom aft is furnished with two bunks, a bureau, and two changing closets, and has generous storage beneath the berths and an enclosed head with shower. The wheelhouse contains an L-shaped settee with a butler's table, as well as a full mahogany table that folds and stows against the bulkhead. The galley is forward and below, with white enamel wooden cabinetry, a stainless steel counter and sink, and several modern conveniences. The guest cabin, with two berths and a second enclosed head, is located forward. The Cleopatra lounge is mounted on the trunk cabin to starboard, and the aft deck space has comfortable wicker furniture and a fold-down mahogany table for dining alfresco.

The description of *Spindrift II*, rather than indicating major improvements, additions, and replacements by later owners, instead is notable for its number of items that have remained aboard since its launching in 1930. The impressive list includes the original Elco lapstrake dinghy and davits, bronze bits and cleats and charley nobles, the mahogany dining table (with serial number), bronze-fitted boat ladders, the ship's bell and brass airhorn, the light fixtures and shades, wicker chairs, and—of course—the original Cleopatra lounge.

"Don and I most love the originality of *Spindrift II*. She has the look and feel of that certain age." Jayne admits that their boat has shown her age in some respects. "Following our first summer of cruising, we eventually discovered that all was perhaps not as it seemed—especially below the waterline."

This discovery resulted in replacing many ribs; refastening the bottom; refastening and recaulking the aft deck; reframing and replanking much of her mid- and quarter section below the waterline; and installing a new starboard shaft and shaft log, fuel tanks, water tanks, and floors.

"While bringing the boat north," Jayne explains, "we dodged an unexpected nor'easter by ducking up the river at Onancock, Virginia, where the locals came to see the boat before we could even tie up at a dock."

Among those admirers, Jayne says, was an elderly gentleman named John Atwater, who told them he had sailed on the boat at the age of seventeen, in Long Island Sound in the late

1930s. He toured the interior of the boat with fond remembrances, amazed at how little the boat had changed from his youth. He explained that while his friends at the time could only think of owning a motorcar, he had been fascinated by boats; he later became a naval commander in World War II.

"His gift to us for allowing him to come aboard the boat was a pair of tiny sepia photos of *Spindrift II* perched atop the twelfth green of the Westhampton Country Club golf course following the 1938 hurricane." The photos show the boat perfectly intact, and there is no damage whatsoever to the green.

Thea Foss

SALTCHUK RESOURCES INC.

Seattle, Washington

The opulence and extravagance of Hollywood during the 1930s is legendary and infamous. The subject of numerous books and films (such as *Sunset Boulevard*), the era that rocketed men and women to unbelievable heights of fame and wealth—only to see them fall into despotism and obscurity, often in less than a mere decade—still baffles us. The great actor of stage and screen John Barrymore is a classic example. Nicknamed the "Great Profile," Barrymore was at the height of his career in 1929 when he commissioned naval architect Ted Geary to design a 120-foot powerboat that Barrymore would present to his new wife, the exquisite actress Dolores Costello. Christened *Infanta* in tribute to their forthcoming child, Dede, the boat would cost Barrymore nearly $225,000 by completion and have every extravagance imaginable—including a grand piano. Yet, by 1938, Barrymore would lose the boat to creditors for a measly $40,000 lien.

Renamed *Polaris* by her next owners, she was commandeered in 1942 by the U.S. Navy, which changed the boat's name to *Amber*. For a brief period after the war, she was used in scientific survey work off the coast of Southern California. She was purchased by the Foss Launch & Tug Company in 1950, named *Thea Foss* after the company's founder, and used as a private corporate yacht.

Like hundreds of other magnificent yachts of the 1920s and 1930s, *Thea Foss* suffered during the Great Depression and the war years. No one knows how the Barrymores' furnishings, artwork, photographs, and other priceless objects disappeared. Holes were chopped in the gunwales at the stern for depth-charge launchers during her wartime use, and cannons were mounted on the teak decks. Marble countertops and lighting fixtures were removed, as was the grand piano. Fortunately, the boat itself was saved. After its purchase in 1950, the Foss Tug Company began a long-term extensive restoration project, re-turning the interior and exterior to the original condition.

Today, it is difficult to imagine that this boat was ever stripped or abused. The exterior brightwork, the teak decks and handrails, and the immense fantail aft decks—both upper and lower—have been returned to a level of beauty that matches the

153

historic photographs from the Barrymore days. The opulence is evident everywhere you turn, from the main cabin with its 1930s-style furniture to the luxury of the lower cabins and master stateroom.

The pilothouse sits forward atop the main deckhouse and includes captain's quarters. The main house has a long passageway starboard, with access to the original formal dining room forward, the galley next, and followed by a large smoking room, which originally contained a fireplace, library, and built-in gun cases. Finally, there is the main cabin, with doors opening onto the spacious aft deck and formal outside dining area.

The teak paneling and joinery work throughout the lower section of the boat are a wood-lover's feast. Beginning with crew quarters forward, which are accessed by either the foredeck hatch or a ladder in the pantry, these accommodations were designed to house four crew members, including an officer's cabin and staterooms for the chef and stewards. Aft of the crew's quarters are the mess and galley; next is the engine room, followed by the main staterooms and three guest cabins. At some point in her history, the original Barrymore suite, located abaft the engine room, was divided into two staterooms, each accessed from the center passageway and each with a private bath. A stairway from the center passageway ascends to the main cabin.

Unique to a boat of this vintage is her magnificent engine room, which still houses the original Atlas Imperial diesel engines. At 275 horsepower each, their polished bronze control levers, stainless steel pushrods, and countless brass gauges are as sparkling as when they were first installed.

In 1987, the Foss Tug Company was acquired by Saltchuk Resources Inc. (formerly Totem Resources), which retained the *Thea Foss* for private events and use by shareholders and company officers. In 1998, the company embarked on a long-term restoration plan that will span several years. Thus far, it has included new interior furniture and wall sconces, as well as more artwork and historical photographs from the Barrymore period. The original cumbersome bridge-to-engine-room telegraph control system has been bypassed, new bow thrusters have been installed, and extensive structural improvements have been made to the bridge and main house. The teak decks will be replaced. The company's long-term plan is to continue the preservation of this historic vessel for the next generation of shareholders.

Much has been written about film legend John Barrymore: his extravagances and failings, his alcoholism, and his inability to manage his massive wealth. As a Hollywood phenomenon, his story is tragic, but his legacy lives on in both his remaining silent and sound films and in the beautiful boat he had built for his young bride and first child. And much has been written about the famous naval architect, Ted Geary, whose magnificent boats recall a period marked by unparalleled style and grace.

Thea Foss	
YEAR:	1930
DESIGNER:	L. E. "Ted" Geary
BUILDER:	Craig Shipyards, Long Beach, California
LENGTH:	120 feet
BEAM:	21 feet, 6 inches
DRAFT:	9 feet, 6 inches
ORIGINAL POWER:	Twin Atlas Imperial, diesel
CURRENT POWER:	Same
CONSTRUCTION:	Steel hull; teak interior, decks, and exterior trim
HOME PORT:	Seattle, Washington

Tomara

DAN AND LYNDA MASON

Bremerton, Washington

Perhaps because wooden boats are made from trees that were once alive, they continue to live and grow as long as they're nurtured and maintained. They are like floating plants that evolve and adapt to their environment: their colors change with the seasons and even their shapes will change slightly. Their wooden structures breathe and emit fragrance, expand and contract, leak and swell. Owners help them change and grow by modifying and improving the layout and design, engines and wiring, plumbing or planking. The process continues as the decades roll past: different owners assume the stewardship, and the boats live in different locations or climates, and sometimes function in different capacities.

Tomara underlines the concept of living and growing, evolving and changing. She was built in 1941 by students at the Edison Technical School of Boatbuilding in Seattle. Today, her makers would hardly recognize her, but they would surely appreciate her. She has been transformed into a trim and elegant cruiser as functional as the intent of her original design.

Commissioned by the vice principal of Edison Tech, *Tomara* was sold immediately after completion to George T. Knight, who kept her at Seattle's Queen City Yacht Club from 1941 until 1960. Named for Knight's two chil-

dren, Tom and Maria, she was documented *Tomara* and has never lost that name.

By 1969, she came under the ownership of Dennis Hostvedt, who kept her at the Bremerton Yacht Club. The son of a boatbuilder and fine-furniture maker, he undertook a total restoration of the boat. Also a professional engineer at the Puget Sound Naval Shipyard and a highly skilled woodworker himself, Hostvedt completely remodeled the interior and added a fly-bridge and teak handrails.

Tomara's interior layout, although still true to Monk's original design, is now more functional and attractive due to Hostvedt's skills and insight. The saloon, entered through the aft cockpit, has excellent headroom, a four-place dinette to port, and a couch-berth opposite. The galley, located amidships to starboard, is open to the saloon; the enclosed head is opposite. The raised pilothouse, with sliding doors on both sides and full 360-degree view, is also open to the galley below, allowing the captain to talk with the mate and guests while underway.

Tomara

YEAR:	1941
DESIGNER:	Ed Monk Sr., Seattle, Washington
BUILDER:	Edison Technical School, Seattle, Washington
LENGTH:	36 feet
BEAM:	10 feet, 9 inches
DRAFT:	3 feet, 3 inches
ORIGINAL POWER:	Chris Craft, gasoline
CURRENT POWER:	Pisces, diesel
CONSTRUCTION:	Port Orford cedar planks, bent-oak frames, mahogany house
HOME PORT:	Bremerton, Washington

Tomara's added flybridge is evidence of Hostvedt's craftsmanship. The curvature of the railing and brightwork trim, the practical addition of concealed rain scuppers, and the gorgeous hatch covers—both forward and aft—evoke craftsmen of long ago. Wooden-boat lovers familiar with the joinery work of the 1920s and 1930s appreciate these rare and sophisticated handcrafted modifications in the age of plastic.

Tomara's fifth and current owners, Dan and Lynda Mason, bought the boat in 1997. "I had known and admired the boat for many years," says Dan. "Hostvedt installed the new diesel engine in 1980, but he never quite finished the boat. Yet, she had always stayed under cover and been well cared for."

A retired chief test engineer for the navy, Dan took over the task of the boat's full restoration, installing electronics, hot water, a shower, and a new transmission; Lynda added new upholstery, carpet, and curtains. The Masons refastened the boat from the waterline down, using more than two thousand screws and plugs.

Every summer, *Tomara* cruises north, as far as the Gulf Islands, the Inside Passage, and Desolation Sound. "This little boat has all the comfort, roominess, and power of a modern cruiser, but the hull and handling characteristics of a sailboat," Dan adds. "Monk could really put the right combinations together for cruising in comfort."

Townley Isle

BARRY AND ANGELLE FAIRALL

Maple Bay, Vancouver Island, British Columbia

Originally named *PGD No. 1*, this beautiful 36-foot cruiser was built for the British Columbia Provincial Police in 1930. They patrolled along the rugged coastline, transporting criminals and doctors—to and from the remote logging and fishing camps accessible only by a small powerboat. Later, she was transferred to the Powell River area, where she continued serving the Canadian government until 1962. According to her current owners, Barry and Angelle Fairall, she was then sold to a couple from Sidney, British Columbia, who named the boat *Mareca II*. Tom Townley bought the boat in 1966 and renamed her *Townley Isle*, after an island off the British Columbia coast named for his great-uncle.

"I purchased the boat from Tom in 1977," says Barry. "At the time, I owned a 25-foot wooden launch, and I was looking around for something a little larger."

As luck would have it, he just happened to be at a marina in Sidney when Townley brought the boat in to list it with a broker. "Mr. Townley was kind enough to show me the boat and take me out on a short cruise," says Barry. "I liked the lines and the looks of the boat so much that I made him an offer right then and there."

Since owning her, Barry has replaced some planks above the waterline

and completely refastened the bottom. However, the boat's exterior is still in its original configuration. "We've made some minor modifications to the interior for creature comforts," says Barry, "but these have always been done with the period of the boat in mind."

Barry and Angelle spend much of their leisure time aboard

the *Townley Isle*, along with their cat, Kibuka. "I hold a Master's Ticket and make my living aboard tugs," says Barry. "Being on the water daily is my life. Just the same, I spend most of my spare time (and spare change) on my boat. She's my sanctuary. My wife and I have cruised extensively through the Inside Passage over the years. We enjoy attending boat festivals and meeting

people who share our passion. I guess that amounts to keeping these old woodies afloat."

Townley Isle's interior layout includes a master stateroom forward, comfortable for two with more than 6 feet of headroom. The pilothouse, with its fascinating collection of antique brass instruments and controls, also includes modern radar and navigation equipment. The galley-saloon is attractive and functional, with the long galley countertop starboard and small dinette arrangement to port abaft the enclosed head. A few steps lead up to the open cockpit aft. The boat is painted gloss white in concurrence with her original design, and trimmed in attractive green canvas and pale green decks. A photograph of *Townley Isle* (when she was still *PGD No. 1*), taken in Alert Bay in 1945 and published in the 1991 issue of *West Coast Mariner*, shows how perfectly original this boat has remained over the decades.

Wooden boat enthusiasts can often see the *Townley Isle* firsthand in British Columbia at the Maple Bay Wooden Boat Festival in Duncan and the Classic Boat Festival in Victoria.

Townley Isle

YEAR:	1930
DESIGNER:	Unknown
BUILDER:	W. M. Menchions, Coal Harbour, Vancouver, British Columbia
LENGTH:	36 feet
BEAM:	10 feet, 6 inches
DRAFT:	4 feet, 8 inches
ORIGINAL POWER:	3-cylinder Vivian, gasoline
CURRENT POWER:	1948 Chrysler Crown
CONSTRUCTION:	Fir planks below water and red-cedar planks above, oak frames
HOME PORT:	Maple Bay, Vancouver Island, British Columbia

Union Jack

Bob and Kathy Jordan

Vancouver, British Columbia

The amazing size and monstrous strength of Douglas fir, the rot-resistant tight grain of yellow cedar, and the abundance of both these natural resources at the beginning of the twentieth century made the Pacific Northwest the natural location for some of the stoutest, most durable, and longest-lasting workboats built anywhere in the world. The availability of excellent woods and the shear size of the growth allowed shipbuilders to design and create workboats that would last for centuries. The *Union Jack*, for example, was constructed from three immense yellow cedar trees cut in the Nimphisk Valley on Vancouver Island. The massive framing structure is constructed of 7-by-14-inch sawn-cedar frames only 7 inches apart. The planks are 3 inches thick, and the distance from the inside of the hull to the outside is a full 14 inches. The hull is planked in 40-foot lengths, as is the deck, also laid in 3-by-3-inch edge-grain Douglas fir.

"A wooden boat is something you grow into over the years and decades," says Bob Jordan, co-owner with his wife Kathy of both the *Parry* (see page 121) and the *Union Jack*. "It becomes an intimate part of your life. Every piece of wire, every screw, every plank is familiar to you. You fashion it to suit yourself. It's like your personal wardrobe."

Bob's long-term ownership of the *Union Jack* has produced just such

a relationship. He knows every inch of her 80-foot length, every mechanical component of her 400-horsepower diesel.

Previously owned by a British Columbia towing and salvage company, the *Union Jack* was removed from full-time service during a maritime strike in 1972. "They parked the boat with no intention of ever using her again," says Bob. "She was wooden, and everything was becoming aluminum or steel. The *Union Jack* had been under constant use since she was launched in 1941, but companies suddenly decided to abandon their wooden tugs—mostly because of maintenance and operating costs. Newer boats took fewer crew to operate, and they required less attention."

As with any period of modernization, the old and reliable are discarded. Most of the wooden tugs were either destroyed or left to sit and rot. Bob recalls that when he and Kathy found the *Union Jack*, she was almost unrecognizable as a boat.

Union Jack

YEAR:	1941
DESIGNER:	Arthur Moscrop
BUILDER:	McKenzie Barge, Vancouver, British Columbia
LENGTH:	80 feet
BEAM:	20 feet
DRAFT:	12 feet
ORIGINAL POWER:	Union, diesel
CURRENT POWER:	Same
CONSTRUCTION:	Yellow-cedar planks over oak frames, fir decks
HOME PORT:	Vancouver, British Columbia

"Her owner at that time had completely covered the boat with sheets of plywood and corrugated metal. You couldn't guess what was underneath all of that. It could have been something like a chip barge. Her interior was a complete nightmare. The engine was seized. Her hull was in critical condition from years of neglect."

Regardless, Bob and Kathy were somehow able to see the potential of this neglected vessel. Eventually, they re-created the amazing boat she is today.

Union Jack is one of the most admired big tugs in the Pacific Northwest. She is both a warm and comfortable year-round home and a mother ship for sport anglers during the summer months. Her large aft saloon is bright with generous windows, cozy from the wood-burning stove, homelike with large green-leather couches port and starboard, and a rolltop desk. Forward of the main cabin is a large combination galley-dining area,

complete with both modern appliances and the traditional diesel cook stove that Bob claims is always lit. Forward of the galley are staterooms, two heads, and a ladder to the small pilothouse perched atop the main house.

The quarters on the lower decks are small with upper and lower bunks, typical of crew's quarters on boats of this era. Most amazing in this classic operation afloat is the organized and polished engine room. It houses the 20-ton Union diesel engine,

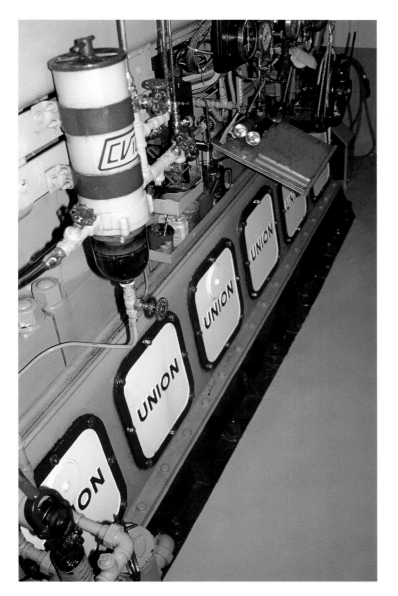

a completely outfitted tool room and workshop, the mammoth pressure tanks, and banks of gauges, all embedded on a solid concrete floor (which functions as part of her ballast).

"Based on her previous logbooks," Bob says, "I can calculate that she has just over 200,000 hours on the engine. I've put 20,000 of those hours on the engine myself."

Bob believes that the *Union Jack* is just now in the prime of her life. Given the constant attention and excellent upkeep she receives, plus the original massive design and construction of her engine and hull, and barring unforeseen tragedy, there's no foreseeable limit to her life span.

Wallace Foss

Dave Walker

Seattle, Washington

The rarity of restored wooden tugboats like *Wallace Foss* is no accident: compared with vintage pleasure craft, fewer tugs were made, and tugboat companies purposely destroyed their boats when they were retired from use. According to the current owner of *Wallace Foss*, Dave Walker, this practice prevented other companies or entrepreneurs from acquiring the boat and returning it to operation, subsequently becoming market rivals. The engines and anything else of value would be removed, and the stripped and empty hull would be towed to an obscure location where it would be sunk or run aground. Such was the fate—or perhaps the salvation—of *Wallace Foss*.

Launched in 1897 and beached by 1911, *Wallace Foss* is currently in tip-top condition and running strong. She has been plying the Pacific Northwest waters of Puget Sound from Tacoma to British Columbia for more than a hundred years. Built in Tacoma's Old Town district, her original power plant was a steam compound engine. During the 1920s, she was acquired by the Foss Tugboat Company, and she served in that capacity until the early 1970s. Her low-profile aft deck and classic tugboat lines still turn heads in every port she visits.

Wallace Foss, named for a family member in keeping with the company's tradition, has been restored to complement her original appearance. She was built by the Blekum Tug Company, intended for passenger service—but at the last minute, *Wallace Foss* was instead finished as a tug. As part of the Blekum fleet, she spent the next fourteen years towing logs, boom sticks, and barges up and down Puget Sound. However, by 1911, she had become a forgotten relic, lying beached along the banks of the Snohomish River near Everett, Washington. In 1913, her deteriorating hull was given a new lease on life by the Foss Towing Company: fitted with a two-cycle, two-cylinder, 100-horsepower surface-ignition engine, she became the first tugboat in the Foss fleet to be powered by an oil engine.

Seven engines, several thousand working hours, and several owners later, Dave Walker discovered *Wallace Foss* for sale as a bank repossession. "I purchased the boat in 1995," says Dave. "I wasn't looking for a boat, but I saw her advertised by a California repossession company, and I couldn't resist making them a very

Wallace Foss

Year:	1897
Designer:	Barbare Boatworks, Tacoma, Washington
Builder:	Blekum Tug Company, Seattle, Washington
Length:	65 feet
Beam:	15 feet, 6 inches
Draft:	5 feet, 8 inches
Original Power:	Steam compound engine
Current Power:	Caterpillar, diesel
Construction:	Oak frames, Douglas-fir planking
Home Port:	Seattle, Washington

Dave recalls that his first major undertaking was to replace the stern section above the waterline from the trunk cabin aft. "We took the boat up to Maple Bay on the east coast of Vancouver Island to have the work done. That first year of cruising was done with a 5-gallon bucket for a head and plastic water jugs for drinking and cooking."

Today, *Wallace Foss* is one of the most attractive vintage workboats on the West Coast. Every summer, Dave and Carol Fennig cruise north to the Gulf Islands, staying out for a full month or more. Bearing a combined total of nine kids ranging from a toddler to college students (and friends), the aft deck of *Wallace Foss* becomes a campground of tents, sleeping bags, and outdoor grills. With her 230-horsepower diesel Cat reliably churning in and out of inlets, coves, and northern ports from Olympia, Washington, to British Columbia's Inside Passage, *Wallace Foss* continues to attract admirers, just as she did throughout the last century.

modest offer. To my surprise, they accepted, and I found myself in the pickle of being a two-boat owner for quite some time."

Since making the offer, Dave admits he has invested endless hours and dollars in restoring *Wallace Foss*. "She'd been sitting on the hard for over six years when I found her, tied up in some sort of legal business. She had been stripped of all functional systems—plumbing, electrical, everything. Her interior was gutted, but she was structurally not too bad."

Westward

HUGH REILLY, PACIFIC CATALYST EXPEDITIONS, L.L.C.

Port Townsend, Washington

The *Westward* was built in 1924 as an expedition vessel, carrying hunters, fisherman, and adventurers from Seattle to the then-remote wilds of Alaska. Pressed into military service, she patrolled waters off the coast of California during World War II. In the 1970s, she spent five years circumnavigating the globe. In the decades since, she has cruised both the Atlantic and Pacific Oceans, from New England to Alaska via the Panama Canal, logging tens of thousands of additional miles.

Today, she still travels the Inside Passage, taking sightseers into the fjords and inlets of Southeast Alaska—after hundreds of thousands of nautical miles, she's still running on her original 110-horsepower four-cylinder Atlas Imperial diesel, leisurely making 8 knots at 300 rpm.

Designed by the famous West Coast naval architect L. E. "Ted" Geary, the *Westward* was built on Vashon Island near Seattle, Washington, for the wealthy young entrepreneur Campbell Church Jr. She was the flagship in his fleet of large cruisers comprising the Alaska Coast Hunting and Cruising Company, which carried passengers on hunting and fishing trips to Southeast Alaska for two decades. Then, like most boats of her size, *Westward* was commandeered for military service during World War II. She was returned to private ownership after the war, and spent the next twenty years

in the Pacific Northwest as a pleasure and charter yacht, with just two different owners. Don and Ann Gumpertz, a cruising couple from southern California, purchased her in 1967.

"The Gumpertzes can really be credited with saving the boat," says current owner Hugh Reilly. "When they bought her back in 1967, they began a major restoration project, which ultimately led to their amazing twenty-five-year relationship with the boat."

The Gumpertzes set out on a five-year voyage around the world, after which they cruised and lived aboard for decades, logging tens of thousands of additional miles between New Eng-

land, the Caribbean, South America, and Alaska—all under power by *Westward*'s original 1924 Atlas diesel engine.

Today, *Westward* is one of two marvelously restored workboats owned by Hugh Reilly's Pacific Catalyst Expeditions. He purchased *Westward* in 1993 and began a refit that included new wiring, plumbing, interior, and galley, and completely rebuilding the Atlas Imperial.

From a distance, *Westward* clearly shows her unmistakable Geary profile, but a description of this boat's current condition and the efforts of both the Gumpertzes and Hugh Reilly must begin in the engine room. It is fascinating to stand amid the heat and rumble of an engine that has been churning for nearly eighty years, looking as clean as the day it was installed.

Topsides forward, the pilothouse is entirely original, with the modest addition of modern navigational aids including radar, depth-sounders, and radios. The main saloon is cozy and attractive, with a large built-in fireplace aft and a long dining table to starboard with built-in seating on either side in the center of the room. Typical of both Ted Geary's design and Campbell Church's requirements, her saloon affords excellent viewing through the large windows around the main deck. The galley, aft of the main saloon, includes a small dinette. Abaft the galley is the large covered aft deck area; covered side decks lead to an even larger deck space forward. This design makes *Westward* the ideal boat for her long voyages through wilderness areas: sightseers can stroll the decks to photograph wildlife, whales, and glaciers.

Below decks and forward of the engine room, *Westward* accommodates eleven passengers with private cabins and heads. Crew quarters are located in the forecastle, accessed only from the foredeck.

Westward is home ported in the scenic shipbuilding town of Port Townsend, Washington, tied up next to her traveling mate, the *Catalyst* (see page 17).

Westward

YEAR:	1924
DESIGNER:	L. E. "Ted" Geary
BUILDER:	Martinolich Shipyard, Vashon Island, Washington
LENGTH:	86 feet
BEAM:	18 feet, 8 inches
DRAFT:	9 feet, 5 inches
ORIGINAL POWER:	4-cylinder Atlas, diesel
CURRENT POWER:	Same
CONSTRUCTION:	Old-growth Douglas-fir planks over sawn Douglas-fir frames
HOME PORT:	Port Townsend, Washington

Index

OF BOATS BY TYPE

The McGraw·Hill Companies

Visit us at: www.internationalmarine.com

2 4 6 8 10 9 7 5 3 1 KHL Singapore
Copyright © 2003 International Marine
All rights reserved. The name "International Marine" and the International Marine logo
are trademarks of The McGraw-Hill Companies.

Library of Congress Cataloging-in-Publication Data
McClure, Ron.
Classic wooden motor yachts / Ron McClure.
p.   cm.
ISBN 0-07-139091-X
1. Yachts. 2. Ships, Wooden. 3. Motorboats. I. Title.
VM331 .M383 2002
623 .8′2314—dc21   2002005093

International Marine/McGraw Hill
P.O. Box 220
Camden, ME 04843
www.internationalmarine.com

All photographs by the author except as noted: page 3, Martin McNair; page 26, Rob Fox; page 32, Bill McKechnie; page 52,
Mike O'Brien; page 56, Mark Daviscourt; page 78, SS *Master Society*; pages 120 and 166, Bob Jordan; and page 153, Shannon Bauhofer.